In 1983, backstage at the [...] Morrison first met. Tracey [...] drummer for The Go-Bet[...] confidantes, comrades and [...] and feminism, books and gigs and rock 'n' roll love affairs.

Thorn takes stock of thirty-seven years of friendship, teasing out the details of connection and affection between two women who seem to be either complete opposites or mirror images of each other. She asks what people see, who does the looking, and ultimately who writes women out of – and back into – history.

~

'The idea of reclaiming women's history is still necessary in 2021 and Thorn, who is a beautiful memoirist, does it with grace and lightness . . . Writing this friendship into history is a gorgeous thing'
Daily Telegraph

'At the book's heart is friendship and feminism, but it is no triumphant tale. Thorn has her claws out, to settle scores on Morrison's behalf and to document the rampant sexism that persists in pop today'
Sunday Times

'Funny, candid and increasingly indignant . . . It may also be the best book Thorn has written . . . *My Rock 'n' Roll Friend* is an act of reclamation'
Herald

'I truly love this book. Thorn's writing is important and necessary . . . Thorn pulls you into the love, to the scenes, heart-stopping moments, as if you were right there, wired in to see the world her way'
Kathryn Williams

'Vibrates with the intensity of deeply felt love and even longing . . . This is both a very specific story of what happens to women in the music industry and a universal one about the people whose impact on us is so much more than the sum of its parts'
New Statesman

Also by Tracey Thorn

Bedsit Disco Queen
Naked at the Albert Hall
Another Planet

My Rock'n'Roll Friend

Friend

Tracey Thorn

CANONGATE

This paperback edition published in 2022 by Canongate Books

First published in Great Britain, the USA and Canada in 2021
by Canongate Books Ltd, 14 High Street, Edinburgh EH1 1TE

Distributed in the USA by Publishers Group West
and in Canada by Publishers Group Canada

canongate.co.uk

1

British Library Cataloguing-in-Publication Data
A catalogue record for this book is available on
request from the British Library

ISBN 978 1 78689 823 4

Typeset in Garamond MT Std by Palimpsest Book Production Ltd,
Falkirk, Stirlingshire

Printed and bound in Great Britain by Clays Ltd, Elcograf S.p.A.

Contents

She will have her own version. I am not the centre of her story, because she herself is that. But I could give her something you can never have, except from another person: what you look like from outside. A reflection. This is part of herself I could give back to her.

– Margaret Atwood, *Cat's Eye*

INTRODUCTION

London, 2020

Dear Lindy,

You won't believe what I've done: me, the quiet one. I've written it down, written *you* down, told all your stories, tried to capture you in the pages of a book. Some people know about you already, or think they do; you're sort of famous. Others have never heard of you, but I don't think it matters either way. This isn't a rock biography, and although the story of your band, The Go-Betweens, is part of the narrative, the real story is you. Or maybe, in truth, the story is you and me, the arc of a friendship, the imprint one person leaves on another.

Do you remember how it began? I do, so clearly: 31 March 1983, backstage at the Lyceum in London. I was in my dressing room sitting in front of the Hollywood-style bulbs surrounding the mirror – uncomfortably bright lights which showed up the tattered glamour of a faded old theatre, dust motes swirling in the air, a worn-out sofa, a carpet that had seen better days, a window that didn't open, stale air.

My band the Marine Girls were about to play a gig supporting Orange Juice. Also on the bill were The

Go-Betweens. I was terrified and out of my depth, unused to dressing rooms, sound checks, gigs in London, all of it. In my second year at university, but still a small-town girl at heart, little more than a child. My band was drifting and splitting, our friendships fracturing, and I felt myself coming apart, beginning to wonder who I was, and what I wanted. Earlier that afternoon I'd been brought close to tears by my first ever encounter with a road crew. Now I was feeling lost and lonely, staring at myself in the mirror. I hated my hair. I hated my outfit. I hated my reflection.

The dressing-room door opened. A breeze. The air changed. Then someone speaking at the top of her voice. Your first words were: 'HAS ANYONE HERE GOT A LIPSTICK I CAN BORROW?' I looked up to see blonde hair and a Lurex dress. A tall, angular woman, who seemed to reflect the light, or perhaps you had your own internal source. You didn't look like you'd ever been scared to go on stage, or felt judged by your own bandmates, or been browbeaten by a road crew. You looked like confidence ran in your veins. You looked like self-belief in a mini dress, the equal of anyone.

I can't remember what I said. I fear that I stared. I tentatively held out a lipstick. Who *was* this woman?

It took me a while to find out. Maybe I'm still finding out. After all the years I realised there was plenty I didn't understand when I started this book. And if you want to know what moved me to start writing it, I'll tell you one more story before I begin. It's the parrots story, and I know you remember it, but maybe you don't quite realise the significance for me. How it sums up so much about who we were, who we are, what it all meant.

It happened in 1987, when I invited you to come and spend a day with me at a spa. You brought along Amanda Brown, who had just joined The Go-Betweens, and together we went to the women-only Sanctuary Spa in Covent Garden.

Opened in 1977, a gift from a millionaire to his ballerina wife, it was one of those luxe-hippy '70s destinations, with a vaguely communal vibe, very much of its time. There were secluded jacuzzis, a sauna and a steam room, and old-fashioned sunbeds. The walls were white and curving, the floors brickwork. Passages and narrow steps led round and back on themselves. Here and there were circular white rattan chairs, and piles of cushions. Wooden footbridges crossed the pools, which were full of koi carp, their mouths gaping open at the surface, begging for food, or gasping for air. Hungry for something anyway. Candles lined the edges of the pools, in a style which was half-Moroccan, half-Japanese.

In the centre was the swimming pool, planted all round with tropical greenery. Ivy trailed down from the ceiling, and a swing extended out over the water, conjuring up images of '70s soft porn, and in fact an orgy scene from the 1978 Joan Collins movie, *The Stud*, had been filmed in this exact spot. Joan had appeared on the swing wearing black lace knickers, stockings and suspenders, although only after loosening up with a few drinks in a nearby Covent Garden pub.

I was faintly embarrassed by the corny connotations of

3

the place, and I wondered what you would make of it, but as we entered you simply shouted at the top of your voice, 'Oh my God, PARROTS!' because, yes, I had forgotten, to complete the rainforest effect, there were a number of brightly coloured parrots flying around.

In the changing room, we put down our bags and reached for our towels and costumes.

'You know, you can actually swim naked here,' I said. 'Some women do. I mean, you don't have to, and it's maybe a bit of a hippy thing, but . . .'

I glanced up into the mirror to see your reflection behind me, and you were stripping.

'I love to swim nude,' you said. Within a few moments Amanda had joined you. 'Come on, it'll be great.'

I rummaged in my bag, looking for something. What? Playing for time. Nudity was natural to you, always easy and liberating, but for me it meant exposure. I'd had very little of it in my life, but I was trying to shake off the constraints of my upbringing and background. In that moment I had to make a decision.

We take off our clothes, and peel off layers.

I think, what is surface, what is depth?

I think of the mirror, and the pool.

I see us clothed and unclothed.

Lipstick, powder and paint.

It was the mid-'80s, and none of us had a Brazilian or a bikini wax; we had full '70s bushes. None of us went to the gym either, or had a boob job, and I was skinny and flat, and you looked at my body, and with your usual lack of restraint shouted, 'Tracey, your tits are TINY!' And I laughed, there being nothing else to do. Something in me began to let go. Was there another way to be?

So there we were, three women from the UK indie music scene, that sexless little world of plimsolls and anoraks, and we were stark naked, swimming in a pool draped in tropical plants, posing with our tits out on the porn swing once used by Joan Collins while parrots swooped and dived above our heads.

A few years later, I did the same again, on a Greek island with Ben, when we drove the length of a rocky track down to an isolated cove, only to find when we got there that it was a nudist beach. A few moments of hesitation, then I picked my naked way across the sand and felt the bliss of being in the sea, the sweet sting of salt and sand, water on skin like a caress. I thought of you that day, and remembered the Sanctuary, and was grateful. One tiny turn of the key in a gradual unlocking.

I know you remember that day too, but maybe you don't know what it meant to me, what so much of our friendship meant to me: how you were a friend to me, but also a symbol.

So go ahead, read it now, and I hope you don't mind what I've done with the story of your life, how I've *used* it: to talk about the two of us, to talk about other women, to talk about how our stories get told by other people, or not told at all. You're at the centre of it all, but as you appear through my eyes.

Maybe all that follows will come as a revelation to you.

PART ONE

BOYS' GAMES

Sydney, 1988

A woman is in a TV studio, being interviewed.
      She's being interviewed because she's the drummer in a rock 'n' roll band.

Beside her sits one of the band's songwriters, who used to be her boyfriend. He's wearing a necklace and lipstick. The interviewer is a geeky-looking guy in glasses, with tinted hair.

The woman is a blonde in a T-shirt, sitting with her legs apart, a short skirt pulled up between her thighs.

The interviewer wants to talk about sexism. And so most of the questions are to the woman. Because sexism is a problem for women to explain, and define, and answer for. We know this.

'Now, Lindy, is there any difference do you think between men and women's ability to express emotion?'

She starts to answer – her face is serious, polite – then she smiles.

'Yes, there's an enormous difference. I think that women can express emotion by being hysterical, and, and, the thing that's said to me most often within the band' – she looks up, thinking hard, leg jiggling slightly, then looks to the songwriter – 'is to stop being emotional, stop being angry, stop expressing it. Because I think we're encouraged as youngsters to cry, and I don't think boys are allowed to, and I think there's a secret language men have which is why you're all so MUCH in power.'

She pulls back, takes hold of her hair and scrapes it into a ponytail, looking down and grinning widely. She seems placatory, but then suddenly her tone changes, becoming faintly angry. Turning again to the songwriter, she says to him in a louder, harsher voice, 'Robbie, are you gonna let me talk, or are you gonna play this game with him?'

The camera pulls back so now the songwriter is in shot too, and she is gesturing between him and the interviewer.

'Are you gonna play this boys' game?'

She slaps her legs.

'OK, let's NOT be serious, let's play boys' games.'

'Now, no, no—' the interviewer interjects.

But it's too late; she's reaching beneath her chair for something and she pulls out a water pistol, and her voice is rising now.

'My God, I'm BRILLIANT at boys' games' – she squirts the interviewer who has a hand up to protect himself and turns – 'absolutely BRILLIANT' – and squirts the song-writer, who also has a hand up. All three of them are smiling, but something has been unleashed, very, very quickly. The atmosphere is electric and alert, all eyes on the woman and what she might do next. The audience applauds.

CUT.

Lindy Morrison was thirty-seven years old at this point. Not young by rock 'n' roll standards. It was near the end of her time in The Go-Betweens. The band would break up soon, having been together for almost a decade. She and the songwriter, Robert, who was thirty-one, had already parted company after several years together, although many people never even knew they'd been a couple. Journalists were embarrassed when they found out. How could they not have noticed? All those song lyrics, for one thing. All those songs about *her*, about *them*. It seemed it was all spelled out there on the records, but who ever knows? Maybe it had been a mistake to have ended up in a band together, but it had just happened that way without any planning, and so now here they were, still connected, still individuals. Part of a group, utterly separate.

Along with a bunch of other ex-pat Australians, The Go-Betweens had lived in London for a few years during the mid-'80s, and Lindy had become my best friend. We had talked and talked, seen ourselves in each other, looked for and found a resonance, a comforting sense of home.

But now the band were back in Australia, and they were trying, still trying, always trying, to make it in the music business. Ambition and enthusiasm had set the motor running, but it had been a longer and harder slog than any of them had imagined. They'd come close a couple of times, but things hadn't panned out, and success had proved elusive, while critical acclaim came easily. For Lindy, who'd had a life before the band and was now consumed by her dreams of a life to come – a life she'd have to create, probably by herself – the engine was running on

11

empty. She must have been so past all this, so weary. So very, very tired of all these boys, all these games.

CUT.

Back in the interview, the woman has a beer beside her now and is smoking a cigarette.

'Now, Lindy, have you turned out, do you think, as your parents would have liked? The drummer in a rock 'n' roll band?'

She blows smoke out, forcefully, looks down, pulls a face, then smiles, wide, eye-crinkling, and laughs. 'No, I don't think so. But then I don't think parents, if they have girls, want them to turn out to be plumbers or train drivers either, else there'd probably be a few more of them around as well. I think they would have preferred me to get married and have children. There's a pretty big tradition of women doing that.'

She grins hugely.

'And, uh, why didn't you?'

'I never wanted to get married, cos I always felt it was a bit of ownership. You know, somebody owns you.'

This is said in a tone of sadness. Or maybe that's wrong, maybe that's projection. It could just as easily be tiredness, or even just sheer boredom at finding herself still saying this, still having this conversation.

The interviewer continues. 'Rock 'n' roll's a pretty macho world, generally. Do you have to put up with a lot of sleaziness or condescending attitudes from men in the industry?'

Without missing a beat she answers, 'I've got pretty good at being sleazy and condescending myself.' She is staring him out, and the mood has once again become confrontational. But who started it? And how long ago?

The interviewer adopts a jokey, sleazy voice and, smiling greasily, he leans forwards, and OH MY GOD, he appears, though it's out of shot, to touch her leg.

'Don't you DARE stroke my leg,' she says with a big laugh, but she means it.

'She's much taller than I am,' he says pathetically.

'Am I? I didn't think I was that tall.'

The mood changes again, in an instant. She picks up her beer with both hands, as though trying to appear smaller and weaker. Maybe this has been a pattern, taking men on, then backing down, taking them on again. The shot pulls back so we can see that the songwriter, the ex-boyfriend, is looking away, disengaged from this whole conversation. He is smiling slightly, at someone we can't see, someone off set. He's elsewhere.

'But do you cop much of that "Oh, she's a woman drummer, she's not the real thing"?'

'Pretty constantly. Now that I'm older it's not as bad, but when I was younger, nearly every single day.'

'How d'you deal with it?'

'I developed a very aggressive way of dealing. I just turned into what I've been commonly called – a bully.'

'Well, for example, imagine I'm saying, "She's no good, she's just a woman".'

'And I'm five years younger? I would have thrown my glass of beer at you.'

She goes to say something else, but the interviewer addresses a question to the songwriter, and realising she has interrupted, she apologises quickly.

'Robert, do you find yourself consciously, or subconsciously, treating Lindy or Amanda a bit differently? Are you more gentle with them than you might be with a guy?'

'Um, no, not really. I think, when we started the band, I always . . . I knew it was going to be a band of both sexes.'

'So, it's no issue with you, really?'

A brisk shake of the head. It's clear the interviewer will get nothing out of him on this topic. There's a digression while the interviewer teases him about sometimes wearing a dress. The songwriter objects – 'I only did it two times' – and in the background she challenges him – 'Robert, that's not true. You used to walk around the bedroom all the time in a nightgown.'

She looks at him affectionately, in a way you could easily mistake for love. Or the ghost of love.

CUT.

When I first met them they were crazy about each other. Or seemed to be. They were allies – another couple in a band, trying to make it work, proving it could work. But maybe it couldn't. It didn't for them.

And this TV interview makes you wonder how far they were allies to each other. She's on her own, fighting this battle alone once again. He's wearing his lipstick and his necklace, but he's the songwriter in the band, so he's not

14

having to defend his corner. Lindy is the one who has to justify herself, account for herself, explain once again what on earth it is she thinks she's doing here.

The conversation is about sexism, and the man is wearing lipstick, but she's the one doing all the work.

CUT.

Now a biker has joined them, and he's been seated next to the woman. He's not a member of the band, or their road crew, or anyone they know. He is there simply to add a spark of controversy – to provoke her and to start an argument. He's her adversary and things are about to get gladiatorial.

The biker is wearing denim jeans, a black Harley Davidson T-shirt and a leather waistcoat. He has sunglasses on his head, a mullet and a huge moustache. He is textbook biker. Cartoon biker.

'Raymond,' says the interviewer, 'what do you think of feminism?'

Good question, yes. We all want to know what Raymond the biker thinks of feminism.

'I'm not really sure what it means. I mean, to me a feminist is . . . it conjures up images of short hair, overalls . . . they don't shave—'

'Wow, come on. I'm a feminist. Look, I shave' – she lifts a bare leg up to him – 'D'you wanna look at my armpits?' – raises an arm to him.

'Are you a feminist?' says the biker. And he leers at her, in a predatory manner.

'Yeah, course I'm a feminist.'

'What does it mean?' he says, in a challenging tone. He's squaring up to her now, looking like he wants a row. Or maybe sex. There's definitely something in the air.

'It means' – she breathes a deep heavy sigh – 'it means that I want to feel totally free as a woman. And not feel in any way oppressed by old attitudes that men have forced upon us.'

Her tone is serious: not angry, not playful, just explanatory. It's courteous of her to pay him the compliment of implying this conversation is worth having. Maybe she's not kidding herself that she'll convert him, but she's aware that this is a TV show, and a wider audience is watching with interest. Maybe it's worth trying to explain to them. Or maybe she just has to speak up on behalf of her sisters. She's been handed the banner, now she's got to lead the bloody march.

The biker interrupts her, ignoring her sincerity. This is a game, and he wants to score points, to win. 'You wanna get on top?'

She looks down. Jesus, we've ended up here again. Nothing I've said has made any difference.

'No, no,' she says, and just for a moment she sounds beaten, ready to quit right here.

But it's not over. She pushes back her hair. She sits up straight. No. Fuck 'em. Damned if I'm gonna let him have the last word.

'Well, if I wanted to be flippant, yes, I'd say I wanna be on top. Sitting down at some bar I'm gonna say, "Yes, I wanna be on top.'" She folds her arms. 'But I'm not sitting at a bar, I'm trying to have a serious conversation.

'So, NO, I don't just wanna be on top, Ray-MOND.'

CUT.

When she gets home from the TV station, Lindy writes me a letter and posts it from an address in Darling Point, Sydney. 'I miss you so much,' she writes, 'you wouldn't believe it, Tracey Thorne.' Spelling my name wrong as usual. It's wrong on the envelope too.

The Go-Betweens are about to start recording a new album – *16 Lovers Lane* – which will be their last. 'Over here, we start rehearsing tomorrow,' she writes. 'Thank god, I've been out of control really.' Everything is becoming complicated for them: relationships are breaking, allegiances forming and dissolving. The letter talks about the 'newfound chumminess' between the band's two songwriters, Robert and Grant, which is causing friction. They'd announced that the two of them were going to produce the new album themselves, asserting control and ownership, which riled the other members of the band. 'Amanda and I actually kicked each other under the table . . . After some argument they proffered that the credit would be The Go-Betweens but they had all the executive decision making. "Oh," we said, because we were both feeling a little awestruck by this no-nonsense mate-ship approach.'

Somewhat bitterly, she refers to the two boys as 'Hamlet and Horatio', although admits they have written some good

17

new songs. 'All love songs except for one of Rob's titled "Clouds", about clouds, I think, but then I'm so literal.'

The letter complains that her sex life has been atrocious; there's been no action at all for months, apart from her bringing home a man called WOLF, who had tattoos and long hair but was doing so much speed he couldn't get it up.

He did play with me. But now when I see him he runs away and hides. I chased him mercilessly, only because I felt like dinner hadn't finished. Anyway I picked up the marching orders which is a good thing as I could never take him home to Mum's, and spending all night in a bar waiting for him was damaging my health. I'm a fool.

The songwriter ex-boyfriend, Robert, is meanwhile having an affair with a woman who is engaged to someone else. Lindy had screamed at him that he was being a pig and he had screamed back, 'You never let me finish a sentence for the whole seven years and at least she listens.'

'SHIT!' writes Lindy.

She is feeling lost back in Australia, having trouble adapting. 'Biting my nails, silly, non-concentrated. I'm glad we're starting work tomorrow, perhaps that will give me something to hold on to.'

And then she tells me what had happened at the TV show.

We did six songs and then an interview over one and a half hours – just Rob and I. The topic – sex roles. They brought in a biker – I mean a really killer biker who said things to me like 'You just want to be on top'

18

and 'You couldn't take me on your back'. It was hilarious. Actually we did very well. I was very languid on camera sitting with my legs apart and my skirt falling between my legs. Flirting with the biker who between takes asked if I would like to spend the night with him after the show, said I would have the time of my life, he could make love all night.

She ends, possibly imagining my shocked disbelieving face – a face I wear much of the time when she is talking to me – with the simple words: 'This is TRUE.'

CUT.

Here are the things I hadn't known when we first met, in London, in 1983: she was thirty-one years old to my twenty, and already on the third act of her adult life. Five years earlier, she'd been living in Brisbane, in a shared house with a bohemian collection of visual artists and musicians, and was the drummer with an uncompromising feminist punk band. Queensland, of which Brisbane is the capital city, chafed under the rule of a quasi-fascist premier, Joh Bjelke-Petersen, and operated more or less as a police state. Political protest was quashed, corruption was rife, law and order out of control. Her band were chased by cops every time they went to a gig, or played one. For young people, Indigenous people, anyone who stood out or who was at all unconventional, harassment and arrests were common. Lindy was caught in the middle of all this and dreaming of escape.

Five years before *that*, in 1972, when I was ten years old and still at primary school, she had been living in a different shared house, with a bunch of actors, all of them politically engaged, progressive and radical. A newly graduated social worker, she was the only white woman employed by the Aboriginal and Torres Strait Islander Legal Service (ATSILS) in Spring Hill, Brisbane. She was out of her comfort zone and out of her depth, but nonetheless committed to the idealistic task of improving life wherever possible for Brisbane's oppressed and mistreated Indigenous population. She shared duties with the activist Denis Walker, who was known as something of an uncompromising firebrand. Inspired by the movement in the US, he had founded a chapter of the Australian Black Panthers. To the shock of Lindy's more strait-laced middle-class family and acquaintances, she was also at this time having a passionate affair with him, which would soon go very wrong indeed.

So when she walked into my dressing room that evening at the Lyceum, I was right to stare. And to wonder who exactly she was. Somehow I was instinctively picking up vibrations which told me that this woman was someone, that she had a story, that she herself was the news.

TERRIBLE JAZZ

Brisbane, 1978

From next door's open windows she can hear a racket, all day long, a racket; the boys who live there have discovered punk. They play the Sex Pistols and The Clash. They play The Slits and Gang of Four. She hears 'Anarchy in the UK' and 'Blank Generation', and she is all ears.

Lindy is twenty-six years old and in a band herself, an all-women group called Shrew, in a classic feminist reclaiming of an abusive term. If they were a punk band they might be called Bitch, or Cunt, but there's a theatrical element to them, hence the Shakespearean connotation, and they're an acoustic outfit, who play terrible jazz. Consisting of saxophone, clarinet, double bass, drums and piano, they tour the lounge rooms of Brisbane, doing covers of 'In the Mood' and 'Chattanooga Choo Choo'.

At the same time she's involved in various forms of street theatre. Over the last couple of years she's been part of the Grin and Tonic Theatre Company, who travel around Queensland in a red truck, performing Shakespeare in school and caravan parks. When it rains, they all lie down in the back of the truck with a tarpaulin pulled over them, and when it's dry they crawl out from under the cover to perform Banjo Paterson poetry. She gets to play both Ophelia and Lady Macbeth, managing somehow to incorporate drumming into her portrayals, and as they finish, 'Lady Midnight' by Leonard Cohen is played over the speakers.

She joins the Popular Theatre Troupe, which is more didactic, playing in factories, driving out to the Utah mines, bringing theatre to the workers. It's all very radical, very agitprop, and her performances earn her an audition with The Pram Factory, an elite fringe theatre group in Melbourne. She is flown in from Brisbane, produces an audition piece which again marries Shakespeare with drumming, and is offered a place on the spot, but in a moment of revelation, she turns it down, realising there and then that she wants a different life, that the theatre isn't where it's at any more. It's music she wants, specifically that music she's hearing from the house next door. It's woken her up, and what she can hear in those punk records, both musically and politically, convinces her that this is what she wants, and that it is all possible, it's something she *can* do.

Suddenly the music she's making with Shrew feels almost embarrassing. 'OH BONDAGE UP YOURS!' comes screaming across the verandah, and the thought of doing another gig where someone's going 'Pardon me, boy', and someone else is twiddling away on the flute, it's unbearable. The wind has changed direction and what had been alternative now seems lame. Girlish even. The boys next door challenge her. They say, 'Why on earth are you playing acoustic music when punk is happening?' This is very much a boy reaction. Unless it's noise, it's not punk. But still, she can see some truth in it, and she doesn't have an answer to their question.

A few years earlier, the house she shared on Dacre Street had had its own dedicated music room. One day she walked into the room and decided to start playing something, but what? She looked at the guitars and amps, and she thought, 'I don't know how to string one of those, or tune it, or what amplifier to use, or what guitar pedal makes what sound. If I pick up a guitar I will have to ask one of the men, "What lead should I use? What's a jack to jack? How does this all work?"' And so, instead, she sat down at the drum kit and felt liberated from all the conversations about technology.

The drums are not the obvious instrument choice for a woman. You have to fight your way into a band anyway. The easiest route is to be the singer. And then there are instruments which are considered quirky, and somehow feminine, like maybe the violin, or the oboe. Keyboards are OK, not too masculine. At a push, you can pick up a guitar or a bass. But to be a drummer? That's really breaking the rules.

Lindy finds the drums appealingly basic and primitive. She realises she can just sit down and bang the bloody things. And it's physical, it's active. There is nothing gentle about being a drummer, nothing passive, yet the concentration required focuses the mind. There's a meditative or trance-like quality about settling into the repetitive groove, and the noise inside your head is momentarily silenced. For an obsessive personality type like Lindy, the drums are both exciting and soothing.

When she first starts playing the drums in the music room, there's a comic artist and jazz drummer hanging around the house called Linzee Arnold, who's ten years older than all of them. Lindy mentions how much she likes playing and he tells her, 'Lindy, you have the rhythm of an ape.' Or maybe he says, 'Lindy, you dance like a gorilla.' I've been told both versions, and they're similar, but mean slightly different things, and one is funny and the other quite cruel. But either way, she has to ignore this. She begins to take lessons. She knows she isn't the best drummer in the world, and it would be so easy to be thwarted, but she is not. Instead of taking the comment as a devastation, she takes it as a joke and chooses to pay more attention to the fact that Arnold also introduces her to the work of Henry Miller, whose books then lead her to Céline and to Anaïs Nin. So if he is trying to stop her in her tracks it certainly doesn't work.

NEVER WEAR SHOES YOU CAN'T RUN IN

In 1978, she needs to find new people to play with, and at the local downtown music hub, The Curry Shop, she hears about a group of girls looking for a female drummer. One day the guitarist Deborah Thomas sidles up to her and says, 'So you think you can play rock 'n' roll?' Lindy turns up to audition for them, with the Premier drum kit she's bought for $100, and before she begins these punk girls give her four Seconals, which she's never taken before, and so in something of a purple haze she drums with them for about five or six hours, going round and round on Tom Robinson Band's two-chord anthem 'Power in the Darkness'.

The band are called Zero, taken from an anarchist feminist paper, and they're mostly lesbians. They're younger than her, eighteen years old to her twenty-six, but tougher than her, shoplifting to pay their way, living together in a huge house filled with other gay women. They push her around a bit, to toughen her up, but they let her join their band. Everyone else she knows is moving to Sydney at this precise moment, but she decides to stay, in her room in a rambling wooden two-up on stilts on Petrie Terrace.

The Zero girls have all assumed punk names. So they have become Irena Zero and Nikki Nought and Debbie Zero. But Lindy doesn't get a new name, and she will remain Lindy Morrison, apart from when she makes an appearance in screenwriter and novelist Gerard Lee's debut, *True Love and How to Get It*, where she is thinly disguised as the character Megaton Monroe – a woman who never knocks, because she is trying to 'crash through the usual barriers which restrict people's freedom of expression', who wears a '50s fluorescent green angora jumper, has a green streak in her white-blonde hair, and can't speak without yelling. On her bedroom wall she has a poster of Marilyn Monroe in black fishnet stockings.

The house she lives in is also immortalised in the novel – 'It's one of those repulsive old colonials with wrought iron railings. The people in before us tore up all the lino to expose floorboards. Makes it cold.' Despite that, it is a very open house, with lots of pot smoking and bed sharing, and its unique feature is the sunken bath, where much entertaining goes on. Another scene in the novel spells out the gritty vibe: 'When we climbed out of the bath I happened to look in the toilet bowl and saw a bloated red tampon.'

The Zero girls are wild and anarchic, and they'll stand up to anyone. Lindy's no wallflower, and she's used to telling men where to get off, but these girls stand their ground when cornered, they fight back. And they have to, because there's trouble on the streets. Just being involved in youth culture, going out for a drink and a gig, is infused in this city at this time with a very specific sense of danger.

The cops can arrest you whenever they like and do whatever they like.

They protest against this shit all the time. Lindy gets her drum kit confiscated for three months by the police, and another time she is arrested at a demo for stealing a cop's watch. It has fallen off his arm while he is chasing them, and she picks it up, then spends the night in jail before the case gets thrown out of court the next day. When Megaton Monroe is getting ready with her housemates to go on a protest march, they have to psych themselves up to face the harassment, the backlash:

"'WADDA WE WANT?" yelled Mega at volume 20.

"EVERYTHING," shouted Pee and Paula.

This was to be their street chant.'

Once Lindy has joined Zero, they start to rehearse every day, in an old warehouse space in Fortitude Valley, where cops and criminals work together running brothels and gambling houses. The band works up a set of covers – songs by Patti Smith, the Velvet Underground, The Slits, X-Ray Spex and The Stranglers. They do an ironic version of the Stones' 'Under My Thumb'. Lindy learns to play the drums very fast and very hard. Inspired by The Slits and Gang of Four, with their stripped-back, angular, spiky rhythms, she soaks up an atypical approach to drumming, developing a style which is not straightforward, and which will become her signature.

But for all their attitude, Zero never get around to writing their own songs, even though they have plenty to say. For some reason they feel they don't have the knowledge. They feel, bizarrely, shut out by the rules, the only set of rules they seem unable to ignore. Instead, they play lots of frenetic gigs, at which they are always the support band, maybe because they don't quite seem like a real band, with none of their own material. What they lack in creativity they make up for in attitude. They are carefree and careless. One time they take part in the Talent Quest at the Festival Hall, and Lindy overhears a group of older musicians complaining – 'That Lindy Morrison, she can't even PLAY!' – but it doesn't faze her in the least. They're only doing it for a laugh, they are a gang of women taking the piss out of the whole thing.

They drive around everywhere in Lindy's red Mini Moke, which she's inherited from her ex-boyfriend Dave Gittins, who will later become Red Stripe in the Flying Pickets. They go to punk gigs and scream at the bands, they play fast and furious shows, one time supporting The Cure. They try to put on a gig in a back lane behind Wellington Street but it's shut down by the police. They play as part of a book launch, with jugglers and street theatre, and the cops break that up too. They go to Newcastle to play a gig at the Star, a real tough-bloke pub venue, and the patrons are shocked by these women, spitting their punk covers at them from the stage. Once again, they have to flee.

Debbie Zero, the guitarist, is young, but wise. She says, 'Never wear shoes you can't run in.'

Lindy makes an impression on everyone who meets her at this point. She is tall and flamboyant, she is loud, she is blonde and attractive, she is like some kind of goddess. People say she isn't like anyone else they've ever met.

This is certainly how she strikes Robert Forster, who will bump into her soon at the rehearsal space on Brunswick Street in Fortitude Valley, used by both Zero and The Go-Betweens, a band which at this stage is just Robert and Grant McLennan, with their fey literary songs and their acoustic guitars. Brisbane is a small music scene, and so everyone sort of knows everyone else, but still, Zero and The Go-Betweens are polar opposites. The political climate of the city means that a lot of the punk music has an obvious focus, but Robert and Grant defy or ignore that template, not seeming to have been influenced or inspired by the same records or events.

The two private schoolboys met and made friends at university in 1977, and their first scene together in this story is a real meet cute: Grant's got three records under his arm, which are Ian Hunter's debut album, Ry Cooder's *Paradise and Lunch*, and Jackson Browne's *Late for the Sky*, while Robert is in thrall to Bob Dylan, Roxy Music, David Bowie and the Velvet Underground. They recognise in each other two typical nerdy boys, both studying literature and drama. Grant has a room full of film magazines, and neither of them are attracted to the aggressive machismo of Brisbane punk. Instead, they're into Patti Smith, Tom Verlaine and Jonathan Richman, and when Robert starts to write songs they reveal a pop sensibility filtered through an academic lens.

And they also reveal a boy who knows nothing about women – literally nothing.

So here we have these two bands, Zero and the nascent Go-Betweens, and they are opposite sides of a coin: one side all feminist activism and rebellion and politics, the other all boyish enchantment with art and intellect and interiority. One side full of experience, the other trapped in innocence. And within each band, two characters, both tall and glamorous, unconventionally but very decidedly attractive, one blonde, one dark, one woman, one man, one Lindy, one Robert, and they meet each other and the whole thing goes KABOOM.

TWO WIMPS AND A WITCH

Our actions around one another were gentle arcs of flirtation: our kisses closing in on the other's lips, hands knocking each other's in the park; it was always, really, a slow chase to the other's skin. When together, it was all loveliness; when apart, the situation was an emergency. It felt as if I were about to flood.

— Naomi Wood, *The Hiding Game*

She sees him first on stage, playing a gig at the Architecture Department of Queensland University. The Go-Betweens' songs are simple in their construction, but he sings them with concentration and commitment. Grant, to the side of him, is all bounce and cheerfulness, playing melodic bass lines and seeming uncomplicated, with his polished shoes and his buttoned-up shirt. Robert, on the other hand, comes across as private, dignified in his bearing, a little eccentric. She's introduced to them both, and Robert is impressed that she is a drummer. She goes to their next gig, sitting on th gazing up at him. Her adoration is obv

If Robert meeting Grant was all about kindred spirits and mutual identification, then the meeting of Robert and Lindy is an attraction of opposites. He reciprocates her interest, he can feel the tug of the magnet, and they start circling each other. He is so beautiful, she thinks, with his long, lanky body, that bashful grin. Something has to happen between them. But the whole project of winning him takes six months. It's like a piece of performance art, a theatre production. The effort that goes into it all, the drama of the thing.

The first night she fucks him – and it is her fucking him, that's obvious – is at Stradbroke Island, where Zero have gone to do a gig. Entirely in character, the Zero girls all listen through the door, giggling and irreverent, as the pair have sex for the first time. They're staying at a nudist beach, and the next day Robert and Lindy emerge, fully naked and holding hands. Robert runs down the beach, and disappears off into the sand and the surf, missing the bus back to town, and having to sleep that night on the shore. She doesn't hear from him for another three days, and she's thinking, 'What the . . . ? Have I lost him? Scared him off already?' He's overwhelmed by his first sex, and is driven half mad with the joy of it all, so happy and grateful that it is both beautiful and sad all at once. Later, he tells a music paper he'd never even French-kissed anyone till he was twenty-one.

She hadn't known he'd been a virgin until a night at someone else's gig. They'd been watching The Apartments on stage, and she was flirting with him, digging for details, prising stuff out of him. He was as vague and elusive as ever, and suddenly a thunderbolt hit her – he wasn't playing games, keeping secret his history of girlfriends. He'd never had any. He'd never had sex. It was like the moment they gave her glasses when she was five years old, and the whole world – which had existed as a blur, something she couldn't quite grasp – came into sharp focus, and she understood, suddenly understood, and knew what had to be done and that it would be OK.

So she fucks him and it's bliss, and then starts the time of them courting, him visiting her at the house on Petrie Terrace. He later writes, in his book *Grant and I*, that he finds the house she lives in – 'a free-wheeling timber house filled with actors, jugglers, ex-prisoners, architects and beauty queens' – to be 'almost TOO bohemian . . . It was a punk residence, but its roots were in the early-seventies counter-culture.' She is seven years older than him and, as he is well aware, 'more outgoing and politically engaged . . . I took a leap and tried to court the most dynamic woman in the city.' It's brave and bold of him, though one day he does say that he wishes she was seven years younger, that they were the same age. Her feelings are hurt, but she shrugs and moves on. What else is there to do?

In every other way, it's a happy time, carefree and irresponsible. Parties take place at the house, and they all smoke pot and have naked baths with anyone who turns up – not orgies as such, just scenes of liberation – and while Robert joins in with all this to an extent, Grant will sit outside in the car and wait for him, unwilling to come into this house of bad women. Robert arrives barefoot, and drinks tea with Lindy on the verandah, and they discuss politics and art. One day, in a scene of complete tenderness, she takes him to the sunken bath and turns on the shower and washes his hair, and he's never had such attention paid to him, he doesn't know anything about anything, and it's beautiful.

Years later, when their relationship is shattering and dissolving, he will write a song called 'Head Full of Steam', and when they play it live on UK television on *The Old Grey Whistle Test*, he's added a few lines that don't appear on the album version: 'Steam may rise / Steam may tear / Can I come to your place / Can I wash your hair.' At the time, Lindy tells me those lines refer to an actual event, which is precious in both their memories, and I feel in possession of secret information, privy to the background details which make up the vivid story of this song.

I am an onlooker, but on the recorded album version, that's me singing the backing vocals on this song. I am both outside and inside this story.

In 1979, Robert and Grant travel to Scotland to make a single for Postcard Records. Lindy moves into their shared house while they're away, sleeping in Robert's single bed, looking at his posters on the wall, writing letters, endless letters. In 1980, Robert returns to Brisbane, he and Lindy reconnect, and pretty soon they move in together. She leaves Zero and joins The Go-Betweens, becoming their eighth drummer. Or, really, their first, as none of the others had settled, or lasted, like she does. It's a big leap, and not everyone is happy with or understands her decision.

With Zero, she's been in a politically motivated punk

band, and The Go-Betweens are decidedly *not* punk and *not* political. They don't have nicknames or slogans or haircuts. They're not a gang or a crew. They're not loud or aggressive. They play acoustic guitars when no one else does. She knows joining them is a risk. They are so different. Just boys. And so square-looking, with their short hair and button-down shirts. Scared of all her friends. Scared of the house she lives in. God, he wouldn't even come inside, that one, that Grant. Sat out in the car. With his books and his film magazines. Furious at her that time he lent her a book and she dropped it in the bath, then handed it back to him, swollen with damp, the pages curled. She couldn't see the fuss. Weren't books to be carried around and read wherever you happened to be, even in the bath? Weren't they to be loved? They weren't just to sit on a shelf and impress girls.

And girls seem to be a mystery to both of them, a different species: alien and attractive, threatening and alluring. Robert writes lyrics about just wanting affection, describing the kind of woman he doesn't want – all earth and lust and sexual threat – and declaring that he 'don't want no hoochie-coochie mama / No back door woman / No Queen Street sex thing.' He writes lyrics about a librarian, or an idealised version of a librarian, half social worker, half nun, not a rock 'n' roll stereotype, sure, but a stereotype all the same. He pines for the female, which he imagines to be exotic, and with which he can't yet connect. He writes a song, 'People Say', about a girlfriend he has imagined, and she is impressive, and it's almost as though he has dreamt Lindy up in his head before even meeting her. When the track is released as a single, in May 1979, there's a thank you on the sleeve to two girlfriends, Jacqueline and Candice, who don't actually exist, but have, in some fictional universe, played 'tambourine and harmonica'. Once Lindy and Robert are together he changes the last lines of the song, which referred to a nonexistent girl packing up a nonexistent saxophone, into a lyric about a very real Lindy packing up her very real drum kit. His songs stop being mere observation and start to reflect lived experience. He has got inside his songs.

Still, he doesn't like songs with 'woman' in the title, preferring to sing about *girls*. Lindy is seven years older than him, very much a woman, and a politicised one.

Robert and Grant are the kind of boys who buy *Playboy* magazine for the Bob Dylan interview inside. They may have written that dedication to girlfriends who didn't exist, but then they became a bit embarrassed about it and decided they wanted a female drummer. They mention *Jules et Jim*, and *The Mod Squad*, threesomes involving two men and one woman. They think all-male bands are too predictable, and they like books and movies with female characters. They're inspired by Moe Tucker of the Velvet Underground – it seems cool to have a girl drummer. Even better, during a brief spell in Paris, they had fantasised about having a French girl drummer! They advertised for '*une femme batteur*', hoping that 'a gamine-faced, stripe-shirted young woman would answer'. Adorable cliché upon cliché.

They feel that a woman might soften the band. And it's hard not to laugh at the fact that they end up with Lindy, who is more ballsy than either of them, full of heart and emotion, yes, but about as soft as a decisive right hook. She's never going to fit in with their fantasies of a chic little French girl, and she's not going to be Edie Sedgwick, and she's not going to revere Dylan like they do without asking some tough questions. As Peter Walsh from The Apartments put it, the leap of faith on Robert's part 'took so much courage it was practically showing off. *What have you gotten yourself into? Didn't you just want some affection?*'

But her joining the band is a leap for all of them. If the boys' desire for her is partly based on a dream, then her admiration for them is more grounded. She can see that they are unique, and they sound like no one else in Brisbane. They are not ideological, and she is becoming tired of the same old politics. Robert rejects the subculture she has come from and says it is just an easy cop-out, that it is full of its own conventions about sex and drugs and art. He talks about a new stance which will reject the old hippy ideals, reject Kerouac, reject punk, and seek instead to drape itself in ambiguity, in a mercurial changeability, in a desire to be fluid and impossible to pin down.

At the time, no one in Brisbane really gets The Go-Betweens. They can't persuade any other members to stay in the band for any length of time. People ridicule them for being so fey. Peter Walsh calls them 'the Choirboys', the way they sing together, cheek to cheek. They don't fit, and they don't impress, and yet one day Lindy walks in to see the two of them playing together, and it is an epiphany to her: she is so struck by the beauty, the cleverness, the lightness and easiness of their sound. Robert and Grant are derided by older musicians who say they can't play, but they say that about Lindy too, and she realises that this music is not beyond her capability and that the three of them could be the perfect combination. She thinks, 'I could have this life. We could be incredible.'

What she sees, before anyone else, is that these two boys have something: ideas, songs, dreams. The kind of qualities that could provide a route out of here – out of this town, this country. Like her, they are ambitious, not so much commercially as artistically. They dream about London and Paris, like she does, and that is a big part of the attraction. Escape is her watchword, and she knows Zero will never want to move anywhere. If she joins this band, it will be her third career change, another throw of the dice to get somewhere, to bring into being the kind of life she craves.

So she joins The Go-Betweens – and at that precise moment they start being a band. It is as a three-piece that they burst into existence, and as a three-piece that they will record their first album, *Send Me a Lullaby*, which will get them noticed by Rough Trade. Lindy chooses the title, and it provides them with an alternative to the words that are scrawled in the record's tail-out groove, and which provide a sarcastic description of the band they are – *Two Wimps and a Witch*.

It is Lindy, Robert and Grant who are the original Go-Betweens. It is *their* band. In the future they might get in backing singers, or keyboard players, or violinists, or sax soloists, or a full-blown bloody orchestra, but the essence remains. They are a classic trio, whatever anyone might say later.

The only fly in the ointment is that while Robert is in love with Lindy, Grant doesn't like her at all. She'll walk into the rehearsal room and he won't say hello. After a few months of that, she stops saying hello too, and from that point on they don't acknowledge each other. This is at the very start, and it's not a good sign, not good at all. It is subtly poisonous, and it will slowly eat away at everything. Bands fall apart due to the tensions of personality conflict, but those same antagonisms can also keep them together, providing a kind of internal tension and friction, a jostling for power, an irritating spark.

So for now, they press on with the business at hand. They leave the big warehouse where everyone else rehearses, as it represents a whole scene they are leaving, and from which they have already been slightly ostracised. They decide to embrace the separation. Lindy makes it her business to start organising them, honing their sound, building a working relationship. She may have lived in a lot of boho houses but her work ethic is far from hippy-ish. The rehearsal room is her province. She finds the spaces, clocks the small ads, phones up the numbers, makes the bookings. Gets them all organised and there on time, and makes them practise.

Practise, practise, practise, she says. It has always been that way, since high school, when there had been a choral competition, and she'd taken it upon herself to make sure that her team would win. She'd spent every spare minute rounding up girls to come and rehearse, chivvying them along. She had been relentless. It was bizarre, inexplicable to her later on, but she had wanted to win so much. And through sheer force of will, HER will, they had won. Now, she applies much of the same rigour about rehearsals to this band she is in. Never thinking of music as a soft option, always knowing it takes effort.

She knows that's all there is to it. It's not magic, it's not a mystery, it's hard fucking graft. Put the hours in, put the effort in. If you wanna get to London and meet your heroes or get to New York and have a chance, you've gotta put the work in. Carrying her little practice pad around with her, tapping away on it, she drives everyone mad, and behind her back they laugh at her. But nothing has ever been handed to her on a plate. She knows effort is essential. She won't necessarily be taken seriously, almost certainly won't in fact. She'll have to earn it, and then earn it again, twice over.

In the flat she shares with Robert, they sit up at night in bed watching the TV which is positioned in front of the beautiful view from their window. The flat looks out over the whole city, and at night when the window is black you can see the distant lights flickering, and they mirror the flickering of the TV set which stays on into the small hours. They watch old Hollywood movies – *Mildred Pierce*, *Sunset Boulevard*, *The Maltese Falcon*. She knows all about European films, the French new wave and Ingmar Bergman, but he is only interested in American culture, and so he teaches her about American films, about Dylan and Tom Verlaine.

Every week his mother makes them a fruit cake, and because they have no money and are on the dole, they live off the fruit cake. The two of them walk around all the time holding hands, and she is twenty-eight to his twenty-one, which never feels weird to her, though her family make snide remarks about cradle-snatching. The flat is in a dangerous part of town, and terrible things happen; they hear fights next door, and someone gets pushed down the stairs. They come home each evening exhausted from the practice room, and sleep in till midday, then get up, eat fruit cake, go to practise, come back and lie in bed watching TV.

At the rehearsal room, the two of them play together for hours and hours, jamming on chords while he works on a new song, over and over again. She learns about how a song develops, and she's there with him while it happens. It's a creative partnership just as strong as the one he has with Grant. The two of them will build up tunes and melodies; she's there while his songs come together, they are locked in a groove, and Grant is jealous of that bond. 'No wonder you're always playing together,' he says, 'it must be so great,' and his tone is envious.

One night back at the flat, while they are glued to the TV screen, someone comes along with a spray can and paints on the fence outside the words ZERO FOREVER. It's a message, and not a very subtle one. Some people think she has made the wrong decision, that she's abandoned her comrades and her politics for the sake of a boyfriend. She has broken ranks, opted out of her world and into his. It's exciting, and it's new, but it's a risk. This better work, she thinks.

41

UNKILLABLE ENERGY

In this moment, Lindy has power. She is their senior, she is Robert's sexual superior, she is here because they want her. Her backstory is more interesting than theirs: she has experience, she has knowledge.

This is a band that looks like it plays by new rules. The boys are certain that they are modern in their outlook, and are proud of themselves for having a woman in the band. They do a gender-swap photo shoot, set in a kitchen. Robert and Grant both wear dresses, like the Rolling Stones did in 1966. Grant's is a shiny polka-dot number with fitted sleeves and a sweetheart neckline. Robert's is silky and flowing and, sitting down, he pushes it up to reveal his hairy thighs, smiling self-consciously. In another shot Robert is slicing bread while Grant does the ironing.

Lindy is the man. She has short, boyish hair and wears jeans, a black shirt and jacket, and a white tie. In each photo she has both a cigarette and a can of beer in hand. She ignores the boys, sticking her feet up on the table to read the paper while they act out being housewives.

The photos don't look entirely sincere – the boys especially look a little bashful, and half-hearted about their femininity. Would it have killed them to put on a slick of lipstick? But Lindy makes a very good man. She looks relaxed and at ease, natural and powerful. Unlike the boys, she looks like she's enjoying herself. Well, who wouldn't? There is always something liberating for a woman about assuming the male role.

But maybe they are just playing at this role-swap business. As will soon become apparent, they don't *really* want Lindy in the driving seat, and they aren't *really* prepared to give up their boy power. Robert isn't a typical alpha male, and he likes to camp it up. He'll continue with this occasional habit of wearing a dress, doing so in the late '80s on a US tour and encountering hostility and bafflement from their indie audience. But on the other hand, even non-alpha males can be conventional about women, and they can fall into the same old patterns of behaviour without noticing, precisely because they think they're above all that.

These photos imply that Lindy is their equal, but there's also a sense that the boys are being self-congratulatory about having a woman in the band. Robert writes later that it was unusual to have a female drummer and 'we were starting to be recognised for the trail we were blazing. We didn't need a prowling front man – we had something else that elicited the same response.'

From the start the boys know that having Lindy makes them more interesting, but later they will start to undermine her role, try to take away her creative input, diminish her power, downplay her importance, and ultimately reframe themselves as having always been a duo. They think they want to be different, but they will end up behaving just like boys in a band.

That title Lindy gives them for the first album, *Send Me a Lullaby*, is inspired by the Zelda Fitzgerald novel *Save Me the Waltz*. And Zelda is an interesting source of inspiration. A woman full of creative urges struggling to find an outlet, she lived, with her husband Scott, a life of drink and carelessness, but battled continually to escape from his artistic shadow, to make something of her own. After an all-out attempt to become a professional ballet dancer ended with a breakdown and a diagnosis of schizophrenia, she was hospitalised. On her release, she took up painting, then astonished everyone by producing a novel, sending it off to a publisher without telling Scott. It represented, as the critic Elizabeth Hardwick writes, another testament to her 'unkillable energy'.

Lindy too is full of unkillable energy. An almost supernatural determination and force of will is embedded in her character, and she will need it. Zelda died in a fire at a hospital, never having achieved artistic equality with her husband. Lindy will blaze and struggle and fight for a long time to get her due.

CHRISTMAS DINNER AND
THE BIRTHDAY PARTY

The Go-Betweens arrive in London in May 1982. *Send
Me a Lullaby* has had good reviews in *Sounds* and the
NME, and they're writing the songs that will become their
second album, *Before Hollywood*. Already, they are attempting
to make their music a little more commercial. Rough Trade
is going to release their next album, Geoff Travis having
been won over from his initial scepticism and coming to
admire the maturity of their songs, the intellectual quirkiness
allied with an emotional heft. Lindy loves Geoff, finding him
unlike most of the men she has met up until now, certainly
Australian men. He's Jewish and cultured and very gentle in
his manner, all qualities which Lindy loves in a man.

London feels like a fresh start, the Old World as a New
World. Buses and taxis in the grimy air are clichés but
beautiful. On the street: faces pinched and wary, eyes
averted. Everywhere: enclosed spaces, a narrowness, a
tightness. Smoke in the pubs, on the tube, in the air. You
breathe in cigarettes and exhaust and drizzle and your
lungs soak it all up, astonished.

Notting Hill in the early '80s is still scruffy, still ungen-
trified. The band settle in a house off Ladbroke Grove,

just round the corner from Rough Trade, and it's the usual shabby, spartan affair. When they're interviewed there, the journalist comments on their spindly kitchen table, which is weighed down with copies of the *Sunday Times*, the *Observer* and the *Guardian*. Lindy says they take all these papers for their arts coverage. They very much don't want to be talked down to as uncultured, uncouth Aussies. Being an Australian in London is difficult at the moment, as Lindy describes in a letter to a friend, Katie Wilson:

> It's so boring over here at the moment with Men at Work, Icehouse and Hunters and Collectors all charting. People come up and hit you on the back and say 'Aussie band – you're doing great'. God, what a lot of shit.

The stereotyping is frustrating. They will find themselves making this complaint many times, often to the UK press.

Various members of Australian underground darlings The Birthday Party are already in London, and the two bands are friends, having recorded a random single together in 1982. They'd found themselves using the same studio – The Birthday Party recording their *Junkyard* album and The Go-Betweens recording 'Hammer the Hammer', a song of Grant's which none of them realise is his first paean to heroin. Going under the name Tuff Monks they record a song called 'After the Fireworks', co-written by Nick Cave, Robert and Grant. The drumming on the track is unmistakably Lindy, who has made it quite clear to The Birthday Party's Mick Harvey that she will *not* be told what rhythm to play.

Being Australians in London now, they are all drawn together, and by 1983, Lindy and Robert have moved into a house on Fulham Palace Road with Nick Cave, bass player Tracy Pew, both their girlfriends and various other people who drop in to stay. A trail of groupies come and go, but it's not girls wanting to have sex with Nick, it's men bringing him drugs. Lindy and Robert are in the top-floor room, slightly separate, and they have a degree of seclusion from all this, but the drug vibe dominates the house. It's always John Coltrane and Miles Davis on the record player, because everyone thinks jazz and heroin go so well together, and Lindy's attempts to play the Carpenters are met with scorn and disdain.

She's also the only one who ever cleans the house. And not only this house. She goes out to clean for other people. Thirty-odd years later, Robert will casually refer to this, saying that 'Lindy, desperate for money and the dignity it confers, was having to work as a cleaner, one job taking her to the house of a Pink Floyd member', an observation that gives away so much more than intended. Meant as a glancing aside, stereotyping Lindy as a bread-head who's 'desperate for money', it begs many questions. Like, why is Lindy the one who has to get a day job to support their artistic career? They are so poor that they have rows about buying butter, or shampoo, or anything that might not be deemed essential. Not everyone in the house is paying their fair share of the rent, but it is only Lindy who decides to take action.

One day, she goes to an agency and signs up for temporary cleaning jobs. Far from finding it demeaning, she finds it intriguing, and spends days in glamorous apartments overlooking the Thames, or huge stucco villas in Holland Park. In one is a round table covered in a collection of snow globes, every single one of which she has to polish. The men of the households will often leave her 50p on the dressing table, as a tip.

She's always had a fascination with the English upper class, and now she is inside their houses, getting a behind-the-scenes look at another way of life. Although after a while it begins to pall, and when she finds herself having to do the ironing for a member of Pink Floyd – when she's come to England specifically to make it herself as a member of a rock band, and believes all ironing to be an idiotic waste of time – she loses patience. In the same letter to Katie Wilson, she writes:

> I know I am an ignoramus for not writing but I have been in such a bad mood for so many months that all you would have got from me is a long whine. It really is a hell of a place to live if it's winter and you're not rich and living with lots of 'blokes' from bands. See you're getting the whine anyway. Besides the fact that I was living with people who despise me . . . It is unnecessary I'm sure to tell you how I feel about them . . . I will be very glad to leave this flat for the tour and to return for a while to Australia. I worked as a cleaner over winter for the rich English. I should have worked as a whore. I fear I'm old and bitter already.

Never one to give up, or give in, she decides to cook a proper Christmas dinner for whoever happens to be around. It will be celebratory, she thinks, will bring them all together, give them something to ward off the gloom, the chill, the never-ending dark that sets in at mid-afternoon every day.

A turkey is hard to come by and expensive, so she buys two chickens. A bag of potatoes, carrots and sprouts, some frozen peas, a box of Bisto gravy powder, satsumas and wine. No one offers an opinion on what she's doing, or offers to help, so she gets to work in the dingy kitchen, and it's as ill-stocked as any kitchen in a rented flat inhabited by junkies. There's a tray, encrusted with years of blackened grease, which will have to do as a roasting tin; a blunt peeler, which slows down the work, until her hands are raw and chapped from the cold water; not enough pans, or lids, so the vegetable boiling is hit and miss; but finally, and somehow, she pulls it all together, and gets a version of a Christmas dinner cooked and ready and on the table, and she calls out, 'Come and get it, everyone!'

There's some shuffling and stumbling into the living room, where she's set up a makeshift table, and they sit down, but she knows that look by now, knows that dumb vacancy on their faces. They've all just shot up. Eyes roll and heads loll. Oh, why not just give up right now, this is hopeless, she thinks, but instead, she serves up the food, passes the plates, blinks back tears.

Have they done this deliberately? Is it an act of aggression? Who cooks Christmas dinner anyway? YOUR MUM, that's who. Is that what this says, that once again she's been too straight, too bourgeois?

One of them falls forwards, face squashed flat against

the tablecloth. The others follow, one by one, slumping in their chairs, or resting heads on elbows. Soon she's the only one left sitting upright, staring ahead at the blasted triumph of the meal: the gravy congealing, the vegetables sitting cold and hard, the unappetising chicken carcass, all bones and grease. What had she been thinking? She pours a glass of red wine, knocks it back, and then another. Happy Christmas, you fuckers.

Lindy smokes a lot of cigarettes and pot, but she steers clear of the heroin, and Nick makes fun of her for this, calls her a hippy. Her not joining in seems to annoy the rest of them. No one likes the outsider, hovering on the fringe, maybe judging. 'Why won't you ever take a risk,' Nick says, 'try something else, some other drugs?' Heroin seems to him to be an almost moral choice: you're putting your life on the line every time. Such courage, such heroism! But to her it just seems lazy. All they do once they're stoned is sit in the living room nodding off to jazz albums. Big deal.

There's loads of heroin sloshing about at this time, and it's quite cheap. And in the drear of a British winter, trapped in the damp of a London flat, heated by three-bar gas fires, and then only if you have a coin for the meter, there is one thing you can say about heroin, and that is that it keeps you warm. You might be starving hungry, and you might be freezing, and you might be looking at pissy lino and grimy windows which barely let through what little light there is, but then you shoot up and suddenly everything is fabulous. She can see why they do it, these poor Aussies, shocked by the dark and the drizzle, cold to the bone, huddling round the spoon and the flame, like Withnail around his cigarette. A blanket of opium, like a hot bath or a warm embrace: shelter from the storm.

And then again, they are drawn to it as *boys*. The male bonding of it all, the ritual of the needle. Piercing flesh, sharing blood. Seeing blood? She's seen plenty already, thanks. She doesn't find it radical; she's already experienced more, and worse. But they paint her into a corner where she's made to look conventional. Tracy Pew overdoses, and each time there follows a ritual that they all seem to *enjoy*, marching him up and down to keep him awake, ignoring her pleas to call an ambulance, regarding her once again as the boring straight one. 'How did *this* happen?' she thinks. 'Back in the house on Petrie Terrace, we were the wild women, the Bad Women. You boys were scared of us. How did you turn the tables on me?'

She's landed in a scene designed by others. She is older, and has gone past needing all this oblivion, all this escape from the self. She doesn't *want* to escape herself; she wants to discover and express herself. Plus, while she can be wild, she is not dark. All this darkness is a drag.

They're nihilists, playing with extinction, where she has already seen violence and squalor, deprivation and power-lessness, courtrooms and jail cells, arrests and beatings. She's been up close to male aggression, guns and knives. These boarding-school boys, flirting with something they can never understand. Think they want danger, want to take a risk? God, they're pathetic, she thinks. It's all pathetic.

But it's a drag being made to feel you're a drag, and

she's driven to petty revenge, it being all that's available. One day she finds some of Nick's heroin on the kitchen floor, and instead of giving it back to him, impulsively and angrily she snorts it. There's only enough for a line, and she's not completely naive; she knows what a line is and what to do with it. It's an exquisite feeling, and fills her with bravado, so that when he comes home and sees that her eyes are pinned, and she is completely stoned, he goes, 'Where d'you get the heroin from?' She replies, 'It's just the greatest thing of all, I found it on the kitchen floor.'

And then she starts laughing, and can't stop. He is furious at her, and stays furious for a long time. 'You stole my heroin!' he'll keep saying, but to her it seems like the greatest joke of all time.

Three months after the Christmas dinner, in March 1983, she walks into my dressing room, calling for a lipstick, and our stories begin to merge, although I have no idea really who she is, or where she's come from. To me she looks like an idealised version of what I want to become. And in some ways she is that, but I have no idea of the journey she's been on to get there. It doesn't occur to me that this woman who seems to be my opposite might in fact be my reflection, that she might have started out very like me – awkward, insecure, isolated – and has had to fight every step of the way to get to where she is now.

I immediately start making her up – half learning about her, half inventing her, the way we do when we first meet people, and our imaginations get to work, either embracing or rejecting them, shaping them to fit the particular needs we have at that particular moment, constructing a person who is just the right shape to fit that person-shaped hole in our lives.

After this first meeting though, I won't see her again for two years.

IT'S LIKE DANCING

Lindy is aware from the moment she sits down behind a drum kit that it is transgressive. She has her legs wide apart, like some dude manspreading on the train, and immediately she is taking up more space, invading that of others, staking her claim. It's indiscreet and immodest. Anyone playing the drums looks cocky, whether or not they have one. She wonders about wearing trousers to preserve her dignity, but then she thinks, 'Fuck that,' and puts on a skirt, and runs the risk of the audience leering up at the space between her legs, and she either cares about that or she doesn't.

Her hands make fists to grip the sticks. She gets blisters on her palms, on the insides of each finger, until she builds up calluses, her hands losing all softness, all gentleness, and becoming those of a worker. She uses tape, like a boxer, around her knuckles. She needs strength in her wrists, in her arms and hands, so she buys a grip strengthener, and she sits and squeezes it at night while she's watching TV. And she needs endurance and stamina so she hits a practice pad, or a pillow, anything that trains her not to rely on the bounce-back energy of the drums. She builds up muscle, her biceps become more defined, her arms strong and sinewy.

When she starts hitting the drums, all at once she's making more noise than anyone else in the room. It's not ladylike, this noise she's making. And she's in charge, whatever the guitarist or the lead singer may think. She's the one counting 'One, two, three, four' to start the song and set the pace. The rest of the band keep to HER time, they move to her beat. If she speeds up or slow down, they have to follow her.

She starts playing, and it's physical, energetic. She gets hot, her hair flies about. Her heart rate increases, she's breathing hard, and she starts to sweat. Then she sweats a bit more. In a hot club, with no ventilation or air conditioning, she really, really sweats. None of this is feminine. None of this is what a woman is supposed to do.

And so, there aren't many women drummers. Think of a number and then halve it. And then again, and again. Then again.

Once upon a time women played the drums. But you have to go back a bit. A long, long way in fact: back before modern pop music, before house and hip hop, before punk and reggae, before glam and prog, before rock 'n' roll, before jazz, before the blues. Before the war, and the war before, and the Industrial Revolution, and the whole modern world – back to the ancient world, to the pre-biblical time of goddesses and priestesses, when they were the ones who played hand-held frame drums at rituals and ceremonies, to honour the dead and to bring the living into trance-like states.

Avant-garde musician Layne Redmond, in her book *When*

the Drummers Were Women: A Spiritual History of Rhythm, traces the history of women in the ancient civilisations of Mesopotamia, Egypt and Sumer holding and playing drums. She notes that for thousands of years and in various cultures women were accepted as drummers, but somewhere along the line patriarchal religions took over, narrowing and defining their roles, formulating rules and regulations about what was and was not considered 'feminine'. Women playing the drums became a transgressive act: abnormal, nonconformist.

Layne Redmond herself, in '90s New York, living in a tenement in Manhattan's Hell's Kitchen and working as a waitress, formed a group called the Mob of Angels, who 'set out to revive the ancient Mediterranean tradition of women's ceremonial drumming', performing ritualised musical events involving processions and circles. It was a radical act: women reclaiming the drums, just as they were reclaiming the night and their bodily autonomy.

There were pioneers, as in everything women have struggled to do, demanded the right to do, been discouraged from doing. Layne Redmond wanted a drum kit as a teenager, but her parents simply ignored the request. It was considered ridiculous. Of *course* you don't want to do that. You'll have to go against all this preconceived wisdom in order to drum. People will say no to you. Hold out their hand to stop you.

Every woman playing the drums has had to really want to. Has had to ignore the word NO. Has had to tell people to FUCK OFF.

And for women who love rock music, are drawn to it for the same reasons the guys are, it *hurts* to be rejected by it. As Lindy West writes in her book *Shrill*, 'In a certain light, feminism is just the long, slow realisation that the stuff you love hates you.'

*

> Lindy was around six feet tall and greyhound slender. She had a wardrobe full of short floaty feminine dresses which she said she wore to act as a counterweight to her macho drumming persona.
>
> – Marie Ryan

The band's second album is *Before Hollywood* and it is Lindy's golden moment. She shines on it, defines the record, brings to the party all her personality and all her lack of convention. Everyone agrees. Even Robert, who can be caustic about Lindy in later years, writes about the album that 'Her drum kit sounded fantastic and she rode every queer-timed riff and rolled on every chorus we put to her. *Before Hollywood* is a master class in creative rock drumming; hers is the distinguishing instrument.'

She loves playing the drums. 'It's like dancing,' she says. Both your feet are working, your hands are always moving, your body is in motion. The strength and power of it makes you feel confident. She knows she's not the best drummer in the world – she started too late – but she can play dynamically and hold the beat, and she works harder at it than anyone else. She's a strong believer in the perspiration-not-inspiration school of thought when it comes to art and music.

And there's a lot of perspiration. At the early Go-Betweens gigs, when they're playing St Kilda in Melbourne, she is sopping wet by the end of the gig, and there is no dressing room for her to change in. So she comes off stage and makes her way to the public toilets, and in a little cubicle, cramped and awkward, she strips off every item of clothing, even her bra, pants and socks, and changes into completely new clothes.

In every way she's an alien, told by men that women can't rock, and that women in bands just cause trouble, and that she'll never be any good however much she practises, but this outsider status ends up being part of her definitive style as a drummer.

Robert and Grant often unwittingly write songs in weird time signatures, and when they bring these songs to Lindy she decides to try to reflect or capture honestly the oddities of their structures. She thinks the boys don't really know how to count their bars, and they have no real sense of timing or rhythm, so it's left to Lindy to literally drum it into them. She is determined not to 'play through' the quirky patterns, and not to straighten them out. She thinks that would be too nice, too boring. Instead, when she is presented with a song like 'Cattle and Cane', written by Grant with a time signature that she identifies as being 'an 11-beat phrase', she preserves all its strangeness, all its distinctiveness. She describes her drumming as providing a kind of counterpoint, rather than a back beat, following the melody in a more lyrical way. The song is lovely in its melodic sweetness, but thanks to Lindy's drumming it is elevated into something much more elusive – a singular piece of music, impossible to pin down.

She hasn't grown up playing foursquare rock music, hasn't learnt the rules, so she doesn't play by them. That doesn't mean she doesn't care. In fact she's passionate about drummers. She loves Hal Blaine, with his simple style punctuated by those dramatic fills, building to grand crescendos. And as much as she loves Wire's drummer Robert Gotobed, she is a huge fan of Karen Carpenter. In New York in the '80s she goes to meet one of her drumming heroes, Gary Chester – 'a total legend', she says – who played on hits for Dionne Warwick and The Shangri-Las among many others. They completely click and she ends up having lessons with him via cassette tape.

When the band complete the *NME*'s 'Portrait of the Artist as a Consumer' in 1983 most of the selections are made by Robert and Grant, but Lindy gets to choose her favourite drum tracks, and they are: Jet Black on The Stranglers' 'Golden Brown', Ringo Starr on 'Come Together', Budgie on 'Typical Girls', Martin Hughes on Robert Wyatt's 'Shipbuilding' and Tony Thompson on Diana Ross's 'Upside Down'.

But, given that she is such an unusual drummer and contributes so much to lifting the band above the clichés of run-of-the-mill indie bands, when it comes to the writing about them, her drumming is often overlooked.

Drumming in general is a low-status role in the world of music. There are endless jokes along the lines of: 'What d'you call someone who hangs around with musicians? A drummer.' Lindy knows this, and she's scathing about it. In a 1987 interview with *Company* magazine she says of drummers, 'They're a great breed of people who understand what egocentric bastards songwriters are. They also understand everybody else's instruments, but nobody understands theirs.'

The Go-Betweens are one of those bands who are reviewed largely on the strength of their lyrics, as though they have published a volume of poetry rather than made an album. The music is mentioned less often than the words, and the drumming least of all. If writers struggle to write about music, then drumming leaves them stumped.

Sometimes the only mention is of what she *looks* like playing the drums:

'Lindy, hovering behind the drums like a ghost of some description.'

'It pays to be pretty. But . . . tonight it's left to Lindy to bear the burden of Go-Betweens visuals . . .'

'Lindy Morrison's fringe sweeps across her eyes as she lashes out a rhythm.'

'We could watch drummer Lindy Morrison's blonde hair lifting in the random breeze blowing on stage.'

I don't have to tell you those reviews are all written by men. When you read what another woman has to say about her, the difference is startling. This, for instance, is from an interview with musician Tracy Ellis:

Seeing Lindy take her handbag on stage and put it down next to her drum kit was a revelation. It's hard to imagine how much of a rebellious act that was. This was at the height of pub rock which, while fabulous in many ways, was also absolutely soaked to the gills in testosterone and alcohol and petrol fumes. When she sat in a vintage frock behind a drum kit and played in her own style, you could feel the winds of change blasting from the stage.

For me, and other women watching her behind the drums on stage, Lindy's presence was a revelation. We knew what we were seeing when we looked at her. We knew what it meant.

I HATE ENGLAND

Since The Go-Betweens arrived in London in 1982 they've been experiencing something of a culture shock. There is a basic personality clash – Australian informality and openness rubbing up against British reserve, stiffness and repression. This clash is nothing new, and is described by Donald Horne in his 1964 book *The Lucky Country*. In Australia, he writes, 'Truth is sometimes blurted out with a directness that can disgust those who come from more devious civilisations.' Australians tend to be hospitable people, he writes, and 'one of the many perplexities involved in the visits of Australians to England lies in the frustration of not receiving the same immediate hospitality'.

Lindy certainly finds this to be true, her forthright manner triggering all sorts of nervous responses in British people she encounters. She had been desperate to escape her home country, frustrated by its smallness, its parochial nature, its lack of progress. In a 1982 interview she says, 'Australia is very conservative musically . . . In Brisbane, if I was to mention Virginia Woolf, or the Velvet Underground, nobody would know what I was talking about . . . That's why we left Australia. There's no aware-ness of ideas. Nobody ever thinks. They're too busy swimming, running, boating, anything rather than thinking.'

But on arrival in England, the band are horrified to find themselves patronised – regarded as unsophisticated, unin-tellectual, a bit of a joke. There are clichés about all Aussies being descendants of convicts, or bush-dwellers, or surfers, and while they don't mind making their own snide remarks about the country they have left behind, it is galling to now have the same put-downs aimed at them.

In part, they are suffering from the 'cultural cringe', a term coined in 1950 by critic A.A. Phillips to describe the difficulty of evaluating art from Australia in comparison to that from overseas, especially Great Britain. Ingrained feelings of inferiority meant that Australian artists in all forms struggled against the notion that nothing they could produce would be as good as the art coming from Europe. And it led many to leave Australia behind, seeking the stamp of approval that success overseas would bring.

The Go-Betweens in 1982 have of course just done exactly this, and have not been at all shy in their dismissals of Australian culture. But now in London, they are seen as representatives of that country and that culture. 'G'day, mate,' giggle the Brits. 'Stick a couple of tinnies on the barbie. Where's your kangaroo? Where's your didgeridoo? Where's your hat with the corks hanging round?'

It's horrendous, and fills them with resentment. They know the music scene is happening here, but apart from that they can't see what London has to be so proud of. Robert thinks it looks like 'the shabbier parts of Brisbane'.

Compared to the city he has left behind, it is 'a flat, never-ending maze-like village'. He hates 'the deadness, the immobility, the closing times, the need to have the right accent'. Both he and Grant gripe endlessly about the poor standard of living, complaining that the place is dirty, and nasty, and unsociable.

And the weather! The winter gloom, dark at four, it's so shocking. The absence of warmth, of light, which seems to them to be a basic human need. This is a band who have defined their music as 'that striped sunlight sound', and now they live in a place where there is no sunlight, striped or otherwise.

As for Lindy, the dislike is more mental than physical. She feels louder and more assertive than everyone she meets, and feels that the band don't fit in. Resentment builds up in her as the years go by, and hardens, until eventually she is letting rip in every interview. A string of insults and counterattacks aimed at the city she'd so wanted to escape to.

I HATE England . . . It's a HARD city, London. The main problem with this city is that it's too expensive to live in the inner city. You NEED an inner city to survive . . . I'll tell you what's wrong with the English. They won't accept any other culture. Just look at the disgusting diet the English have . . .What is so GREAT about being English? . . . that mentality is a residue from the days of having an empire . . . The British are just an unfriendly, unwelcoming people. They're the worst audience to play for.

One interviewer says to her that all the Brits know of her culture is 'lager, Paul Hogan and Australian rules football', to which Lindy replies, with an accuracy that can only have silenced him where he stood: 'It's the same for Australians. We see your soccer violence, Benny Hill and Margaret Thatcher. We think you're pretty barbaric too.'

By 1983 the UK music scene is falling in love with The Smiths. The Go-Betweens are their label-mates on Rough Trade, and so they play a gig supporting them at the Venue in London. It's one of those moments when two bands seem close, with some shared style and ambitions, but then suddenly one pulls ahead of the other and is soon far in the distance, out of sight, passing unimagined finishing lines.

The Go-Betweens are building up to their third album, and want to go to New York to record it. A budget is discussed with Rough Trade, but there are some constraints in place. *Before Hollywood* hasn't sold very well, so there are limits. Then The Smiths take off. 'This Charming Man' is a hit, and the band become Rough Trade's darlings. The Go-Betweens fly out to New York for a gig at Danceteria, and meet Geoff Travis who is there with The Smiths. He has bad news. There is no money for The Go-Betweens' album, even though The Smiths are supposed to be saving Rough Trade's financial bacon, and so the band are off the label.

Some of the bitterness about being Australians in London is suddenly brought into sharp focus. They are being set aside in favour of Morrissey, who plays up to a stereotype of Englishness, but is also a much more flamboyant and boisterous onstage performer than either Robert or Grant. For all their comments about English reserve, The Go-Betweens' live shows are fairly sedate affairs, with nothing like the unrestrained euphoria of a Smiths gig. People don't really dance at their gigs; the band don't seem to be at all wild or hedonistic; there's a danger that the relationship between band and audience could remain quite distant and polite. Respectful rather than passionate. They need to find a way to connect.

Morrissey is writing about a recognisable British landscape, full of recognisable characters, while Robert and Grant's songs are full of defining Australian imagery. In *The Lucky Country*, Horne describes 'the haunting landscapes of Australia – the great herds of cattle drifting across vast, shadeless plains . . . the deep green of the cane fields', summoning up one of the band's most famous songs, 'Cattle and Cane', twenty years before it will be written.

So is the band's material doomed to render them incomprehensible to a European audience? They sound romantically exotic, poetic and mysterious to English ears, but might this 'otherness' put limits on their appeal? A band needs to bond with their fans: to be the crowd's mouthpiece in some way; to articulate what they can't; to seem to have all the same thoughts and feelings and experiences as the audience, but be able to express them better.

It's just another problem to add to what are becoming the difficulties of establishing themselves as contenders. They go to a studio in the South of France to record the new album, *Spring Hill Fair*, and immediately come up against the new tyranny of the recording studio – the widespread use of click tracks and programmed drum parts. The mid-'80s pressure to have hits doesn't sit comfortably with the angularity of this band, the lack of rhythmic regularity. The single, 'Bachelor Kisses', despite having one of The Raincoats on backing vocals, is straighter than much of their early material, more foursquare, more obvious in its construction. The person with most to lose at this point is Lindy. Her role as drummer is diminished when the emphasis is more on rigid time-keeping than performance, or dynamics, or freedom. And without Lindy drumming in her distinctive way, the band are not so much themselves.

As always, pop has discovered a set of new rules which apply to everyone – even an angular art-rock band who write songs about libraries and cattle stations, set to drum patterns whose cardiac arrhythmia echoes all the anxious palpitations of the lyrics. Robert will write later: 'suddenly we were face to face with eighties recording hell.'

Spring Hill Fair will not be a massive success, and even some of their admirers look on it as a failure of a record, perhaps trying to be something it could never be – falling short of being commercial, while abandoning its natural niche.

Lindy herself is clear about what is wrong. 'The reasons *Spring Hill Fair* was such a disaster was due to the relationships in the band at the time. They were fucked. There were little power struggles going on all over the place. We were a neurotic mess. It was a horrible experience, and it shows.'

And so, the years of struggle begin.

PART TWO

PART TWO

WHAT IS THE PROBLEM?

The thing about being very young, as you are, is
   the permeability
Of one person to another.
   – Hannah Sullivan, 'You, Very Young in New York'

You appeared before me in the mirror, and then, just as quickly, you vanished.

The 1983 meeting is vivid and clear in my memory, but then there's a gap. Two years pass. I leave university and go on tour and become a minor pop star, and you and the band record two more albums and go on tour a lot and don't really make it as pop stars, and then before you know it, it's 1985, and there's a simple entry in my diary: 'Thursday 30 May. Lindy and Robert 6.30.'

But how have we become friends? That detail is lost to me.

There are many specifics which draw us towards each other, similarities and differences.

We're alike and unalike, but I think we see each other, and being seen is everything.

We're both ambitious. We live in London, though we come from somewhere else.

You're a drummer, I'm a singer, but we read, we like films.

We complain about men, desire men, move in a world of men.

I feel like I'm following you, or like you're my sister.

We've shaken off our mothers.

And you've done so much. I don't know the half of it.

Suddenly my diary is full of you.

We go to the cinema together: 'Tuesday 4 June. Lindy at Electric Screen – 7.35 Come and Get It, 9.30 Committed'. You get me to video TV programmes for you: 'Tuesday 18 June. Video Hayley Mills programme for Lindy. 7.30 BBC1 The Time of Your Life.' You come round for dinner: 'Saturday 6 July. Lindy and Robert', and we go to gigs: 'Tuesday 23 July. Robert and Lindy, Woodentops at Mean Fiddler.' I come to see you play live: 'Friday 16 August. Go-Betweens Merlin's Cave.'

By August 1985, we are friends enough to go on holiday together: 'Saturday 24 August. Holiday, Balcombe, Sussex. £120 1st week, £90 2nd week'.

Ben and I rent a cottage deep in the countryside and invite friends to stay. You and Robert are the first to arrive, along with a journalist from the *NME* and his girlfriend. Followed by the current members of our band, our A&R man and a photographer. On paper it looks like a rock 'n' roll fortnight, but there's also a literary, nostalgic quality to it all.

It's a fifteenth-century house, close enough to the railway station at Balcombe that friends arrive by train, lugging their suitcases up the lane. The same family have lived here for generations, but now they've moved into the much bigger main part of the house and rent out the old, smaller wing. I've never been in a house like it before. There are worn oak floors, open fireplaces and a bare brick chimney. Tatty sofas, ratty rugs and stuffed bookshelves, enveloped in a layer of ancient dust. An all-pervasive smell of woodsmoke, even in the summer, and at the far end of the sitting room, a stag's head mounted on the wall, ominous and creepy. Upstairs there are doors that aren't to be opened, an attic that connects to the main house, and floorboards that creak at every footstep.

In the evenings we cook huge pots of student-style vegetarian meals, risottos and pastas, and we drink heavy red wine at summer body temperature. We read E.M. Forster novels and argue about The Loft. One day, we go for a walk together – me and Ben, you and Robert – and Ben and I have a fight. He storms off in a huff, marching way ahead, while the three of us trail behind.

I say to you, 'It's not the fight that's the problem, it's how to move on after the fight, how to get back to normal,' and you tell me years later that you always remembered that, thought it was very wise, and very true in many situations.

It's not the actual fight, it's how to get over the fight.

The owner of the house is an elderly lady who, as a young girl, had been friends with the daughter of one of the Bloomsbury crowd. Charleston House, the gathering place of Vanessa Bell and Duncan Grant, Virginia Woolf and John Maynard Keynes, is not far away, and much of the old house here is decorated in the same style. There are painted panels in the bathroom, and borders in the bedrooms, decorated cupboards and DIY friezes. I am a huge fan of the Bloomsbury crowd so this is catnip to me. I feel I've landed right in the heart of a liberal, free-thinking, intellectual, unconventional milieu, and that it's exactly where I belong. Although, when we stay at the house again, months later, and invite the elderly lady owner to come and drink a glass of Beaujolais Nouveau with us, she says, *'Beaujolais Nouveau?'* in a tone of incredulity that there could be such a thing, that it even has a name, and looks at us as though we are just the sort of people to drink it.

And you, Lindy, you embody for me this unconvention-ality that I'm determined will define my life. Robert buys a cape, and wears it sitting in the garden, the picture of eccentricity, the artist in his element, but your moment of rule breaking makes more of an impression.

The next time we all go for a walk, you stay behind to explore. Behind the old house you find some outbuildings, including a barn whose doors we have never opened. Inside is a pile of dusty old cases and trunks, which you open to find a stash of letters, hundreds and hundreds of them, and, without thinking, you start to read them. They date from the Second World War, and are from a man – the son of the house? – to his father. He is in Germany, and the descriptions in his letters are so compelling that you're drawn in, can't stop reading.

Later on, when we return from our walk, you can't wait to tell us. 'I've spent the whole afternoon in a barn reading wartime letters and it was the most beautiful thing!' You are entranced by it, having been lost in the past, energised by the thrill of uncovering a secret. You expect us all to be entertained and impressed by your daring, but the news is incendiary. Everyone is shocked and scandalised by what you've done, Robert especially, thinking it a gross intrusion into someone else's privacy, and instead of admiration there follows an argument about the rights and wrongs.

You are dumbfounded, and don't understand at all. 'I haven't harmed anyone. No one said we couldn't go into the barn. The letters weren't locked away. I haven't broken and entered, or stolen anything. All I did was LOOK. Anyone would. What on earth is your bloody problem?'

I'm somewhere in the middle and I keep my mouth shut. I can see that it was perhaps wrong, but not for the first or last time, I'm excited by you. I wouldn't have done it, but you've done it for me. I think the others are being disingenuous, up on their high horses claiming the moral high ground and pretending not to be curious about the details.

You and Robert end up having a row about it, possibly because there is a precedent. We don't know it, but you've done this before. Years ago, when the two of you were first a couple, you'd moved into Robert's room while he and Grant travelled to Scotland. In Grant's room next door, you found letters discarded in the bin, and read them. They were from a friend who admired Grant's work, and so, once again, you couldn't see the problem. 'They were

IN THE BIN for God's sake. They'd been thrown out!' But again, when you told everyone, the reaction was disgust and anger.

Robert will write a song called 'Bow Down', which is a tribute to your forcefulness, but it opens with a line about you opening his mail, and it being a kind of stripping, a pulling apart of himself at the seams, an ultimate revealing. So maybe this incident frightened him.

Anyway, I learn some things about you that day. You're drawn to a story. You're more romantic than I'd imagined. But you're no respecter of privacy. This might be a red flag to a person embarking on a new friendship. I should see it as a clear warning sign. Instead, I hear a starting pistol.

Thirty-five years later, I ask if you remember this incident and I am thrilled that you do, vividly. I had thought perhaps I was exaggerating its importance, but to you too it was a moment. And there is more to it than I had known at the time. You tell me that the night after the row about the letters in the barn, you had broken into the locked attic of the house, finding there a collection of clothes and costume jewellery and vintage sunglasses, and were only dissuaded from stealing a pair of the sunglasses because of the fuss the night before. You tell me that you still regret not taking them.

Then you go on.

'What I didn't tell you about the barn though, is that I DID actually steal one of the letters. I've still got it. I couldn't resist. I thought, these letters are just gonna be lost, no one's going to save them, no one's going to publish them. And so I took one, 'cause then there's one letter saved. So yeah, I stole someone's property. When I told everyone about reading the letters, they were all furious and disapproving, so I lied about taking one. But I stand by it. Those letters will all be damp and mouldy now, and the one I've got is probably the only one that still exists.'

You scan and send me a copy of the letter. It is type-written, and at the top of the page are the words, 'From Oflag VII B', which puzzles me, so I look it up online and discover that this was a German prisoner-of-war camp for officers in Bavaria. I read some of its history – tales of escapees who are recaptured and sent to Colditz, the story of its liberation in 1945 by the US Army. And the extraor-dinary fact that Benjamin Britten wrote a piece of music dedicated to 'Richard Wood and the musicians of Oflag VII B', a microfilm of which was smuggled into the camp for the prisoners to sing.

So you did indeed read, and then steal, a letter with a history, rich and fascinating. I don't know if that makes it more right or more wrong, or makes any difference at all.

You tell me you're still not sorry about any of it. And when I remind you of your previous history of mail pilfering, you start laughing, and then can't stop laughing.

'It's hilarious. I mustn't have very clear boundaries.'

Well, do any of us? We're hypocrites about such things. We devour biographies which only exist because someone opened a box they weren't supposed to, or read some letters and diaries they were expressly forbidden to read. We respect privacy up until the point where we want to hear the end of the story, and then we tell ourselves that the story justifies everything. Is anything out of bounds?

Maybe you and I are the kind of people who can't look away; who can't obey an instruction not to read; who can't resist, can't stand back, always want to know more. I appear to be more discreet than you but in many ways I aspire to your levels of indiscretion. I'm never going to purse my lips at you disapprovingly if you're telling me a good story.

TOO BLOODY MUCH

Still, as friends we are opposites in many ways. Dionysian/Apollonian, and it's obvious which way round. I like to think that I'm very rational, am in fact wedded to the notion of being so. I don't seem to have noticed that I have to work hard at maintaining this fiction, and that there is effort involved in trying to live my life according to the rules of order and reason. Perhaps because of the effort, I am constantly drawn to those who do the opposite. Am I looking for balance? Or to be completed? Or contradicted?

You seem to me to be ruled by emotion, to act on instinct, to idealise honesty and openness. You are loud where I am quiet, excitable where I try to be calm, unguarded where I am reserved. You can be outrageous – I'll tell you something flippant or in confidence and it will come out loud and drunk in public. And that annoys me, sometimes infuriates me even, mostly because I am embarrassed.

But you look everyone straight in the eye, while I am glancing up from under my fringe, and you ask direct questions in a way I've never heard before. You have a habit of beginning every personal question with an unapologetic, 'SO'.

You'll say:

'SO – how long have you been having an affair?'

'SO – what is it that's good about sex with him?'

'SO – have you always hated your mother?'

'SO – do you think he might be gay?'

I am sometimes horrified, but full of envy, and try to work out whether I can use any of this approach myself. For a while I experiment with using the opening 'So', borrowing your style, hoping some of your content might rub off on me. But in truth, it doesn't suit me. My caution intervenes, my protective instincts kick in just when I'm near the edge. I'm drawn to the flame, but ultimately I back away from it.

When it comes to describing you, everyone uses the same phrase: a force of nature. I do it myself in *Bedsit Disco Queen*: 'as for Lindy, well, she was a sheer force of nature, an Amazonian blonde ten years older than me, unshockable, confrontational and loud'.

Your friend Marie Ryan says in the liner notes to a Go-Betweens box set: 'She was a force of nature, brash, opinionated and loud.'

Writer Clinton Walker says: 'Lindy, is, as we know, this force of nature, and she's very attractive in that, you know, and she can be a FUCKING NIGHTMARE.'

Peter Walsh doesn't use the actual phrase, but comes close:

Lindy Morrison. Her great, upending, tumultuous, machine-gun laugh . . . SHE SPOKE, IF NOT LIVED,

EXCLUSIVELY IN CAPSLOCK, a Klieg light in a roomful of 40 watt bulbs. Describing her quickly exhausted all possible weather metaphors. Gales of laughter, gusts of enthusiasm, a storm of personality that broke in every room.

An interview in *Hero* magazine says: 'Lindy Morrison is an excitable girl. Some would say volcanic.'

So. It's clear that you make an impression. You're like a tornado, or a hurricane, or a tsunami, or an earthquake, or a volcano, or a lightning strike. And what do they all have in common? They're amazing and impressive, but also terrifying and destructive.

Tara Westover, in *Educated*, describes her grandma as a force of nature, and then adds: 'To look at her was to take a step back.' We are daunted by forces of nature. Frightened at the same time as we are awed. They make us wary.

When the phrase is used about a woman especially, it implies real danger. So when male writers describe you in the music press, they characterise you as a 'difficult woman'. You fit a stereotype – that of the awkward, problematic woman: too loud, too brash, too argumentative.

The boys in the band, Robert and Grant, are portrayed as the calm, reasonable ones – intellectual, brainy, writer types. Maybe a bit shy, a bit awkward, a bit lacking in social skills. But nothing that makes them difficult. But there it is, scratched into the tail-out groove of the album: *Two Wimps and a Witch*.

Robert writes a song about you called 'As Long As That', full of images of lightning, and thunder, and windows banging shut, in which he says, 'think of someone and double it'.

You are not just natural, you are MORE than the normal – supra-normal, above and beyond. Even compliments make you sound extreme. A person could be overwhelmed or overpowered by you. I'm reminded of the quote from Richard Burton where he describes his first meeting with Elizabeth Taylor: 'She was unquestionably gorgeous. I can think of no other word to describe a combination of plentitude, frugality, abundance, tightness. She was lavish . . . She was, in short, too bloody much . . .'

Who wouldn't want to be described like that? On the other hand, if you were a man, would your personality characteristics attract such notice? They are amplified because of your gender. You are loud, but so are many men. You are opinionated and indiscreet, but so are many men. You break the rules of femininity.

Men are scared of you, and I quite like that. Though I wonder if it is as much fun for you. The stories they tell about you make you sound mythic, but terrifying. A legendary bitch. There are worse things to be.

You are older than all of us – me and my other friends, the boys in The Go-Betweens, all the blokes you encounter. The mid-'80s UK indie scene is full of boy-men, and dominated by infantilised sexual politics, and you stand out like a beacon: more politicised and more cultured. You just KNOW more. I always think it is as if Aztec Camera had Germaine Greer on drums.

And you remind me of Germaine in so many ways. I watch *Town Bloody Hall*, the film of her in 1971 arguing with Norman Mailer about feminism, and I see you there. Germaine looks like a rock goddess, with her dark tousled hair, sleeveless vest and necklace. She glowers and smoulders like Patti Smith or Cher. I've read her books, but you have lived through the period when they were written.

These journalists who write about the band, they don't emerge covered in glory from their encounters with you. I read their pieces and I think, such wimps. Hadn't they ever met a woman before?

SOME PERVERSE LIBRARIAN

> Out of the ash
> I rise with my red hair
> And I eat men like air.
> — Sylvia Plath, 'Lady Lazarus'

I tell myself that you find it exciting to scare men, but I wonder whether a lot of the time it is just boring. They scare so easy that you'd think they must be making it up. But no, they really do seem to be as easily shocked as your schoolteachers, or your parents. Journalists have trouble writing about your drumming, but when they try to describe your personality they fall to pieces, revealing more about themselves than about you, thrilling themselves with their fantasies of how dangerous you are.

Here's a quote from the *NME*, 1986:

Lindy Morrison is The Go-Betweens' drummer. Maybe she was born with it, or maybe it was acquired doing what's traditionally a man's job in the most macho non-Latin society on earth, but Lindy has a notoriously hard head. A braver soul than me would tell you that she drinks, swears, and threatens too much (no, not for a woman, for ANYONE!)

Here's another one, from *Sounds*, 1988:

(She has) a reputation as the kind of woman who would come up to you in a disco, grab you by the throat, push you against a wall and shout, Hey! Are you ignoring me? I wanna talk to you.

You drink and swear, and it looks threatening, it hints at violence. You are a tall woman, but still a woman. To these men, your strength of character implies actual menace. Sometimes you act 'tough' in response to being discarded from the creative process, or in response to *actual* threat. You fight your corner, defend your art, and your role in the band. But as so often when a woman speaks, all that is heard is rage, and it takes shape in the mind of the listener as physical aggression. Your words are heard as blows.

You say to me, '*I remember seeing this journalist at an event, and he was so scared of me that he saw me and he actually COWERED, he cowered . . .*'

You are described in *Hot Press* in 1990 as resembling 'some kind of perverse librarian, who you could easily imagine stamping your hand instead of the book – just for the look on your face'.

My band the Marine Girls have been described as looking like we'd break your arm before we'd let you break our hearts, and these things sound like compliments, praising women who are no one's fool. But there's an implication that demanding equal space and respect makes you the aggressor. These journalists, they are either scared of you, or they are pretending to be. And they shift the blame for this on to you.

In an interview with *Company* magazine in 1987, you describe the cruel behaviour meted out to you in the past: 'I started off thinking that girls playing in bands meant things were changing – but they're not . . . I still get people saying to me, "Do you really think you can play as well as a bloke?" . . . When I first joined The Go-Betweens in '79 the crew would make comments about the way I was sitting on my drum kit . . . really quite crude.'

When you do an interview at the office of *Sounds* in 1983, the journalist describes you 'slinking past the Page Three birds on *Sounds* wall . . .' These are the days when the offices of the alternative music press have topless pin-ups on the wall. Your toughness is a responsive toughness, forced upon you by circumstance. You say, 'Queensland is where we're from and that's the most conservative state in Australia. You soon build up a violence towards the world because the world is violent towards you.'

At school, you hadn't been rebellious, just enthusiastic. Too loud, too engaged, too bloody much. It wasn't seemly, or ladylike. You were elected head of house by your peers, but not made prefect by the teachers, and it was the first time in the school's history that that had happened. Your peers got you, but for the teachers, you were too much.

You'd already heard it at home from your dad. 'You'll

never get a husband,' he tells you, 'unless you're demure. You've got to be more demure.'

So later, the way journalists write about you, making you sound scary and threatening – it is all part of the same repeated message, tired and worn but not yet done with. These are the rules you're breaking. Keep your voice down, wait your turn.

How disappointing, how frustrating, to find that the world of rock 'n' roll operated along the same lines as a '6os private girls' school in a small Australian country town. Your dad wanted you to be more demure, and so did the *NME*.

We're talking in 2019 and you say to me, 'I felt that I had to be that way – I had to be very tough to withstand the kind of sexism that I was meeting all the time, during the late '7os and early '8os. I also felt an obligation – this might sound strange – to protect Robert and Grant. Because they really were timid – they were not able to stand up to men the way I could, 'cause they might get hit – and I even said that to them sometimes – just leave it to me 'cause I'm less likely to be hit than you are – if we were in dangerous situations. Someone had to be tough, and it was me . . .'

And I ask you, 'How do you feel about all those descriptions, all those men describing you as so scary?'

'Yeah, that one journalist, I was pissed off about something in that interview, and the next time he saw me, he ran away, like I was gonna hit him or something . . . But I did wear the pants in the band . . .'

'And what about being called Two Wimps and a Witch?'

'Oh, I never minded that – I think the boys come out of it worse – I thought it was funny; it's like reclaiming an insult, turning it into something defiant.

'I mean they were all men for God's sake. I was always surrounded by men: it was men in the van, men in the dressing room, men in the rehearsal room – and that's how it was – just men.'

'Were you EVER interviewed by women?' I ask, and you jump up, saying, 'Yeah, there's one. I've got one here in a book – hang on, let me find it.'

One, I think.

So these journalists, they ask Robert and Grant about their dreams and influences, about their backgrounds, about the bands they love; they all go on about Dylan and the Velvets, and they share interests and history and context, and we know who these boys are, and where these boys fit; they are placed in context, in a continuum, while you are treated like an anomaly. And if only they'd wondered more about *your* context, if they'd asked about your dreams, your past, they'd have got some brilliant stories.

Like, for instance . . .

TAPESTRY

Brisbane, 1973

The night she drives the three men from Brisbane to Cairns – a 1,000-mile overnight journey in a large white Ford, with her the only driver, and the three of them asleep in the back – is the night she wins their respect. Sixteen hours it takes, through the darkness and the fields of sugar cane, and the only thing she has to keep her awake is Carole King's *Tapestry* on cassette. She listens to Side One, starting off with 'I Feel the Earth Move', and ending 'Way Over Yonder', and then she flips the tape over for 'You've Got a Friend', and 'Will You Love Me Tomorrow?', and as Side Two finishes, the final words ringing in her head, those man-written lyrics about being a natural woman, she goes right back to the start again, until she knows every word, and every beat of every song.

Sixteen hours, and when the men wake up in the morning, they are shocked to find themselves in the north, in Townsville, and they look at her differently, like she's earned her stripes. She is exhausted, sweaty and drained, and they need to find somewhere to stay, but every motel turns them away. There are no rooms available, because

89

while she is young and blonde and white, the three men are black.

There is so much going on here. The woman, naive and inexperienced, but with a core of courage and determination that fuels her through the drive. The record, that quintessential soundtrack of the '70s feminist: Tin Pan Alley songs, written by a Jewish woman, then made into hits sung by black women, and now re-recorded by the Jewish woman who wrote them. Anthems of liberation and longing, earthy hymns to emancipation, the stripped-down arrangements echoing the nakedness of the sentiments. Carole King's piano and voice ringing out through the night, fighting to be heard above the engine noise.

And what of the men? Their sleep displays what? Trust? Confidence? But then, on arrival, they are the ones turned away at the motels. There is no entitlement or power here. These are men who are treated as second-class citizens in their own country, and who've come here to fight another battle, in a long drawn-out war.

They are Denis Walker and two Indigenous elders, and they are making the trip in order to establish a North Queensland branch of the Aboriginal and Torres Strait Islander Legal Service (ATSILS), which has been operating in Brisbane since 1972, with Lindy as its second full-time employee. She's in her early twenties, and fresh out of university, where she studied social work. A middle-class white girl radicalised by her studies, and by the times themselves. A private school-educated doctor's daughter, who'd grown up in another world, which was actually only the other side of town, and with privilege, despite never recognising it as such, having never known anything else.

Since 1968 Joh Bjelke-Petersen has been Premier of Queensland, and he is an oppressively authoritarian conservative. Or maybe that's being too polite. 'A cunning, right-wing hillbilly dictator' Robert Forster calls him; 'a bible-bashing bastard' according to Prime Minister Gough Whitlam.

His regime is both corrupt and violent. When his popularity dips, he turns to strong-arm law-and-order tactics to enforce his will – most strikingly during the anti-apartheid protests against the visit of the South African rugby union team, the Springboks, in the winter of 1971. To prevent demonstrations in Brisbane, Bjelke-Petersen declares a state of emergency, seizing unprecedented and near-limitless powers for the authorities. In defiance of this ruling, a huge crowd of activists and protestors, around 2,000 in number, gather outside the hotel where the Springboks are staying.

Lindy is among them, and she witnesses the moment when the protest – on Wickham Terrace, the very street where her doctor father has his private practice – turns violent. The police have had their numbers reinforced by cops brought in from rural areas. The crowds are chanting, 'Paint them black and send them back,' and in response these 'brownshirts' shout back, 'Paint them red and shoot them dead.' It is a terrifying scene: the police lay into the crowd with batons; Lindy is running as fast as she can, while friends are knocked down; she's trying not to stumble and fall, she's too scared to stop and help anyone who has fallen. It is a turning-point moment, and not just for her. 'It radicalised everybody,' she says.

But marching against the apartheid state in South Africa is one thing. It raises the obvious question: what about Australia? Anyone with a political imagination can see the parallels between apartheid and the complete lack of racial equality in their own country.

Since 1788, when the British arrived, declaring the land 'Terra Nullius' – 'no one's land' – the Indigenous people of Australia, who apparently did not exist, have been displaced, imprisoned and massacred. They have fought back, time and time again, but it isn't until the late '6os, partly inspired by the civil rights movement in the US, that the struggle develops into a more organised movement for land rights and self-determination.

Lindy herself has grown up in a house on a huge plot of land, and she hadn't understood the meaning of that, or appreciated its value. It had been her childhood home, a lovely place by the river, but it is LAND, and she is learning lessons now about its significance. She joins in with demonstrations and marches, feeling inflamed, but also helpless. There must be a way to make this more than just a part-time protest? In her last year at university, she is offered a student placement working for ATSILS. It's her chance to try and make a difference.

And so in August 1972, she climbs the steps to the second floor of the building on George Street where ATSILS have their office, and stands in front of the desk of the Aboriginal and Islander field officer, Denis Walker. He is rock-star skinny and dressed in tight black jeans, an unbuttoned fitted black shirt and black boots. He is doodling on a bit of paper, and smoking a fag, and doesn't even look at her. Lindy mumbles something about being a social work student, who doesn't know much about Aboriginals, but who wants to join the team and help in some way, to which he replies: 'You could help by not calling us "Aboriginals" – we're blacks.'

LOVE IS GEOGRAPHY

Denis is about four or five years older than twenty-two-year-old Lindy, and she's never met anyone like him. For a start he is gorgeous, very handsome, in a rock 'n' roll kind of way — aviator shades, tight black clothes, a little bit Phil Lynott, a little bit Hendrix . . . *he looks amazing, unbelievably good-looking* . . . It doesn't hurt that he is unpredictable and exciting too. Sometimes those words are code for other, more hidden characteristics. He is volatile, prone to anger. Sam Watson, who started the Black Panther Party with Denis, writes of him, 'He had this violent, incredibly charismatic persona.' And God knows he has every right to be angry a lot of the time, and about many things.

He wears his hair in a short afro, and after a while exchanges the black gear for a suit with purple flares, and the motorbike for a white Ford. He talks revolution, quoting Eldridge Cleaver's *Soul on Ice*, Huey Newton, Malcolm X and Frantz Fanon. Every day he and Lindy go to the Magistrates Court and apply for bail for whoever has been arrested the night before outside the black pubs in Petrie Terrace, Spring Hill and South Brisbane. If they can get the clients out of jail, they take them back to the ATSILS office, where Lindy investigates their social and economic problems, and the lawyers try to sort out their legal issues.

After a while they let Lindy join the 'Pig Patrol'. This had started from the idea that instead of bailing people out, they could stop them getting arrested in the first place. A group from ATSILS wait outside the pubs at 10 p.m., and when the police arrive to arrest unaccompanied black men and women for drunkenness, they bargain with the cops, intervening on the men and women's behalf, and offering to drive or escort them home, or somewhere safe . . . *Oh, it's real Wild West country, you can't imagine* . . . They have to use all their wiles, but the Pig Patrol is a direct intervention which makes a difference, and arrest rates fall.

It is a leap though, for a sheltered, middle-class white girl, fresh out of university. She is filled with anger at the racism she sees everywhere, and equally filled with ideals. She is out of her depth, but burning with rage at the system, the injustice and the cruelty. Sam Watson talks about how every time he ran into a certain cop, that cop would 'pull his gun out and play Russian Roulette with me'. She'd had no idea how deep the racism was in the place she lived; that there are only certain pubs where Indigenous people can drink; that there is one pub where people sleep in the basement, many people, in appalling conditions.

Hanging out in places where violence is commonplace, she becomes both radicalised and a little desensitised. She toughens up, feels useful . . . *there are black pubs and white pubs, and I'm suddenly drinking in all the black pubs. It's where I learn to play pool* . . . She's doing social work over the pool tables, passing on valuable information about how to get the benefits they are entitled to, how to get kids back out of care, how to get a place to live.

It is in this atmosphere of defiance and righteous anger that she falls in love with Denis Walker. For a year, they do everything together, are an invincible couple. They spend all day driving around Redhill and South Brisbane checking out families in need, and all evening travelling round the pubs to make sure that people are safe . . . *'Love is geography,' my dad had always said* . . . and they are thrown into each other's orbit, sharing the same space, some of the same experiences. The physical closeness works its magic, binds them together.

But there is inequality there too, and that's the enemy of love. Right from the start, he had challenged her. 'D'you think you can handle this? Think you're tough enough to stand up to the pigs, and to the white racists in the government?' He tells her that she has come into *his* world, and now she'll have to play by those rules. He tells her she'll have to choose which side she is on, and be pretty sure about it. He is loved by some, because he is uncompromising and unapologetic in his demands, fierce and passionate as any activist has to be. But others are more wary of him and hint to Lindy that he has another side; you need to watch him.

He gets angered about the slow pace of change, is tired of waiting, and she understands that, so maybe she is slow to listen when people whisper warnings . . . *He always says there can't be a separate women's group, that it would break things up* . . . He is insistent that white people shouldn't take over the organisation, like they always take over everything, and so he holds control of it firmly in his grasp, and one night, when a decision goes against him he takes out his fury by driving the two of them in his car at 100mph across the William Jolly Bridge on the wrong side of the road, and she knows the only thing to do is to sit very quiet and calm and not make things worse.

YOU WILL WALK AWAY

All this time Lindy is living in a shared house in Dacre Street, just up the road from the cemetery, with a crowd of actors, musicians, social workers and students. It is a '70s hippy house. Nice middle-class grammar-school kids gone rogue. Sex, drugs, art, politics – the usual. Revolutionary talk and theatrical antics. Geoffrey Rush is in the kitchen, using the serving hatch as a proscenium arch, acting at everyone through the window. Bille Brown is in the lounge room conducting Mahler, reciting Shakespeare until he is moved to tears, whether at the beauty of the words or the sound of his own voice is not clear. When there are tropical downpours which flood the whole area, Geoffrey gets them to turn the dining table upside down and they enact the story of the *Titanic*.

Lindy's feminism is now firmly entrenched, and so when a guy comes up to her in the pub, the Royal Exchange, where all the young theatrical revolutionaries and musicians hang out, and asks, 'Can I buy you a beer?' she replies simply, 'FUCK OFF, YOU SEXIST PIG.'

Lindy reads Kate Millett's *Sexual Politics*, and starts quoting from it all day long. She'll begin sentences: 'Well,

Kate says . . .' and, 'Y'know, Kate says that . . .' until one day, at the house on Dacre Street, her friend Trevor Stuart can't stand it any longer and yells at her, 'Stop quoting Kate Millett. You've got to have your own ideas, you can't just live off someone else's' – and then he takes the book and throws it up on the roof. All the women scream, 'YOU CAN'T THROW KATE MILLETT ON THE ROOF,' and so he climbs up and retrieves it, until an hour or so later, when Lindy starts annoying him again, he throws it back up there, and it stays put for a few days.

Everyone is nude all the time, because it's so hot, and because it's the '70s. They sleep on top of the bedclothes, and still wake up steamy and sweaty. Lindy and her friend Diana play bridge in the nude. They go swimming nude. There's nudity in all the theatrical shows they take part in, or go and see. When they're not nude, Trevor and Geoffrey like to dress up as women, and when visitors arrive they pretend to *be* women.

Trevor and Diana are a couple but the rules of engagement aren't clear. One day he returns home and asks, 'Where's Diana?' and is told that she's downstairs fucking some Maoist. Another time he and Lindy have sex, just the once, and when years later she tells Diana, the news is received very badly. It seems there were rules after all, even if no one knew what they were.

Everyone's off their heads all the time, and fearless about what they'll do, what they'll try. They jump in a car, six of them in a four-seater, the air thick with smoke, their heads thick with smoke, off to see the latest Stanley Kubrick film, not thinking about the police, even though the police are everywhere, and they know all about it, have all had their encounters. Trevor had got coshed on the head at that Springbok protest.

The Dacre Street house is where Lindy first picks up the drumsticks, though not that seriously at first. She has her records too, and her liking for them carries some of the obsessional quality she brings to much of life. Trevor comes home one day to find a guy pleading with Lindy. Turns out he's a neighbour. 'I've just come over to ask you, please stop playing the record you're playing, you've played it thirty-six times in a row. It's not even that good, and I've counted, you've played it thirty-six times.'

Lindy replies, 'But I love it, I really love it.'

The record is Carly Simon's 'You're So Vain'.

These two worlds aren't separate, they are intermingled. Everyone at the house shares her politics, and friends from ATSILS hang out there too. In emergencies, she puts up whole families until a place can be found for them.

But there is perhaps an uneasy peace between these two worlds, and it doesn't hold for long. Her time working for ATSILS comes to an end at the same time as her affair with Denis, and the ending when it comes is abrupt and violent, though no one wants to talk about it in detail. All I have is a version of events, with impressions, not details; it's a kind of dream, full of ferocity, but lacking clarity.

It goes something like this:

Some people are in a house, Lindy and Denis among them. An argument breaks out between two men, prompted by an insult.

The argument turns vicious, escalates into a fight, and an act of extreme violence is committed.

Someone has a bottle, not sure who.

Someone gets stabbed, not sure who.

Blood on the floor, blood everywhere, and she tries not to see, or to remember.

An ambulance is called, but the police arrive first.

Lights, hammering, panic, shouting, chaos, so much fear.

The victim goes to hospital, and a sickly calm settles on the house and the awful night bleeds into the days that follow.

The victim recovers.

The story makes headline news.

Lindy's parents are distraught and horrified.

She herself is left shattered and dumb, never fully certain what has happened or what it means.

Everything comes to an end: her time at ATSILS, her relationship with Denis. Has she failed? He had said to her during their affair, 'You will leave all this behind and walk away because with your white skin you can. I can never walk away; none of us blacks can walk away. But you will, you will walk away – just because you can.'

And in the end, yes, she does, she walks away. Maybe he had been right all along. The gulf between them is too wide, and it becomes unbridgeable. Or the bridge they have tried to build suddenly collapses under too much weight. She talks to her friend Trevor about the inevitability of their break-up and he says gnomically that 'there was more than one truth'. Meaning, she thinks, that politics alone can't account for the complexities of the human heart, or explain to her what went wrong.

She leaves ATSILS, and takes a job for a year with the Department of Children's Services, working with the same Indigenous families. But now she has more power to improve individual lives, most significantly getting children out of care and back living with their mothers.

She knows she is making a difference. She's learned so much, and is no longer the naive, idealistic student, no longer trying to be the white saviour. In just a couple of years, she has learned that while she might not be able to change everything, she can change *some* things; it's better than nothing. She's accepted a degree of compromise about work and about the world.

But while compromise is part of her character, it's not the whole story, and she's also an ambitious dreamer, a would-be artist. She is full of curiosity about the world, and already feeling stuck in the small town of Brisbane and the small world of Australia.

She isn't the kind of person who's going to let herself get stuck. And now there is another possibility opening up.

The actors have announced that they are all heading to Europe.

SPANISH STEPS

1975

On the deck of a ship sailing from Fremantle to Singapore, she lies with her friend Diana, both of them whacked from the dope they've been smoking, aware only of the great deep ocean moving darkly beside them.

They've had to spend a few days in Adelaide, where they've stayed with Maoist friends who judged them for not being political enough. Rigid and intolerant, they were the kind of people who had decided not to have kids because a fascist coup might be imminent, and Lindy and Diana were happy to escape. Now they have a week onboard this ship, and they pass the time smoking, and playing in a chess tournament, where Lindy is told she can win if she sleeps with her Yugoslavian opponent. She declines, and is the runner-up.

By the end of February they have made it to London and a flat in West Hampstead. The city is damp, cold and drizzly, its inhabitants closed off and impenetrable; on the streets they pass crowds of people who seem blank and expressionless. But they are here for the culture as much as anything else, and so they embark on an orgy of consumption.

They see *The Tempest* with Paul Scofield, and Bergman's *Scenes from a Marriage*. They see the musical *John, Paul, George, Ringo . . . and Bert*, but it is mediocre nostalgia. They see some awful clichéd political theatre. They visit Regent's Park Zoo, take a boat down the river to Tower Bridge, and go to Madame Tussauds. They both start attending a clown and improvisation class.

In March it snows, and they go to the British Museum, and to see Fellini's *Amarcord*. The strain of being cooped up in a small flat, with bad colds, is telling on them, and so they head down to Canterbury and Dover, then back to Kew Gardens, the fair on Hampstead Heath and Highgate Cemetery, and jazz at the Royal Festival Hall.

They go to Brighton, and see the Pavilion, the pier and the pebbled beach. They go to Speakers' Corner. They see *La Règle du Jeu, Monty Python and the Holy Grail* and *Tommy*. They see *The Norman Conquests* by Alan Ayckbourn, Buster Keaton's *The General*, Bergman's *Smiles of a Summer Night*. They see Fassbinder's *The Bitter Tears of Petra von Kant*, and then more Bergman: *Persona* and *The Rite* and *Shame*. They see Pinter's *No Man's Land*, with Ralph Richardson and John Gielgud at the Old Vic, then go to Oxford, and to Stratford-upon-Avon where they see *Henry V*.

The weather is so cold it makes them flinch. It's supposed to be spring. In May, they decide to leave England and visit the rest of Europe. Diana goes first, to France, where she meets up with Trevor. He's bought a converted ambulance in Paris. It has four beds in it and they intend to use it to drive around Europe, but when it breaks down a third of the way through France they abandon it in a field. From there, they hitchhike to Rome where they are meant to meet Lindy. They have written to her at a Post Restante saying, 'We'll meet you on the Spanish Steps between 12 and 1 when we get there, on any day, so wait for us'. Every day for a week or so she goes and sits on the Spanish Steps and when they finally turn up she is furious at having been made to wait so long.

But now it's early June, and they need to repair this friendship before going off on their travels. Diana confides in Trevor that she is worried about the lack of love between her and Lindy, to which he replies, 'Lindy wants desperately to be free but may not know what that means or entails.' The two women have a long drunken talk and resolve things. Lindy says she has been eager to escape from Trevor and Diana in order to be herself. But when Diana and Trevor part at Rome station the two women set off together.

They go to Capri and Sorrento, and to Florence, where they visit the Accademia, the Pitti Palace and the Uffizi. They hitch to Bologna and then to Venice, where they hang out in a hostel with students talking about Communism and architecture. They go to the Lido, which is full of fat Italians and Germans in front of their striped tents, and to a jet-set party in Kit Lambert's Venetian Palace, where, as Diana writes in her journal, there is 'much wine and decadence'.

They hitch to Treviso, and then on to a mountain pass where they stand for a couple of hours, reading about Van Morrison and Joni Mitchell, finally getting a ride with some Italians to Canazei. They hitch to Bolzano, where a rich Belgian takes them to Innsbruck and buys them a roast beef lunch. They hitch to Zurich, to a sleazy hostel, and they go to see *The Third Man*. They hitch to Interlaken, and then to Grunewald.

They hitch to Montreux, where Lindy wins forty francs at the casino. The next day, two millionaires invite them onto their boat, and later to an apartment to stay in the sauna room instead of having to brave the Swiss night. One of them is the owner of Montreux's only disco. They go to the jazz festival, where they see Rory Gallagher and Loudon Wainwright, then spend another day on the sailing boat with Montreux's jet set.

They hitch to Grenoble, to Perpignan, near the Spanish border, and then they fall asleep in a truck and arrive in Barcelona by mistake, where they hang out on the Ramblas with some US servicemen who 'went to Nam and became a man'.

They hitch to Madrid, but in the middle of the night, in the back of a truck, there are groping hands and heavy breathing, and they decide to sing hymns all the way in the hope of warding off unwelcome advances. When the truck stops for a coffee break they jump out and run for a hotel.

They go to the Prado, and to the red light district, and to a bull fight which is 'horribly exciting'. They spend a night at a disco where Lindy tries, in slow loud English, to explain feminism to a man she has just met. They sleep in Retiro Park.

They hitch to Granada, but the truck driver asks for a blow job and when they refuse, dumps them in the middle of nowhere. They hitch to Nerja, and meet Romanian twins. After a night at a bar and disco with flamenco dancers, they each have sex with a twin. They hitch to Málaga, then to Algeciras, where they take the ferry to Morocco, smoke hashish in the Medina, lose themselves in the crowd, and get groped a thousand times.

They take the bus to Casablanca, where Lindy gets the runs, then a bus to Marrakesh, where they smoke and watch snake charmers, clowns and acrobats. A guy asks Lindy out, she puts him off, but later he reappears and a fight ensues, which ends with the man spitting on her.

They drive to Fez, in a van which breaks down, so they walk to the Algerian embassy for visas. All this with both of them suffering from diarrhoea. It takes seven hours to cross the border into Algeria – and finally to a camp site. A few days later Lindy is still ill, and properly depressed, fearing that she might die in Algeria. When she recovers a little, they drive to Tunisia, but then become ill again.

It's August now. They've been travelling in a van with some boys, but finally they separate from them, and it's a relief to get away. Life in the van has held few comforts, and their travelling companions were darker characters than had first been apparent. Lindy is still ill and depressed, so they fly to Rome and get a connection to Athens, only to find that it has changed – it's become expensive and full of hippies.

They go to a Greek hospital for jabs, then to the port at Piraeus, where they take a ferry to Ios. They meet some Aussies and stay a week or so, then sail to Paros, and then back to Athens, and sleep in lice-infested student accommodation.

They hitch to Delphi, sleep on a hostel roof, visit some

ruins, and join an Aussie van convoy, but find it parochial and insular, so they make their excuses and hitch to Yugoslavia. They take a bus to Skopje, then hitch again, but are driven off the road onto a muddy sidetrack by the randy driver. After escaping, they spend a paranoid night in someone's cottage.

They go to Dubrovnik, where Tito's name is branded into the mountainside, and then hitch to Rupa. It's a tiny village, with few hotels, so they sleep against a haystack in a field. When Lindy hears a thrashing noise she is convinced two men are converging on them, and shouts, 'Grab your bag and run!' Diana isn't convinced, so she sits tight. In the end she is proved right when they hear the unmistakable noise of a horse snorting nearby.

They hitch to Munich, and then start out for France. A racing-car driver speeds them 300km to Paris, where they stay for a week at the Shakespeare and Company bookshop.

They see Greta Garbo films: *Mata Hari, Ninotchka, Anna Christie, Anna Karenina*. They read Pushkin, Turgenev, Gogol. They see Brando in *The Wild One*. They visit Sacré-Coeur and Montmartre. Finally, at the end of October, they head sadly back to London.

They've been travelling non-stop for four or five months. It being the '70s, when these things were still possible, they find an affordable room in Swiss Cottage, in leafy Strathray Gardens. Two single beds, a cooker with one burner, no television. They keep the butter cold on the window ledge outside. They see *Rosencrantz and Guildenstern, Giant, Claire's Knee, Hiroshima Mon Amour*, some Buñuel films. They listen to Lou Reed.

London is still a low-rise, soot-blackened city. The streets are full of Zodiacs and Minis. Cars, and everything else, come in shades of burgundy, pale blue and mustard. Donkey brown and bottle green. In the charts are Led Zeppelin and ABBA. The Who and Demis Roussos.

One night they go to see Bruce Springsteen at Hammersmith Odeon, and although Diana describes it in her diary as just 'good raunchy rock', this is the seminal gig that people still talk about. Bruce plays 'Thunder Road', 'Tenth Avenue Freeze-Out' and 'Born to Run', and does a nine-song encore, and Lindy falls in love with 'Born to Run', playing the album so much she practically drives everyone from the house.

On 11 November they get a call from a friend telling them the news from Australia – Labor Prime Minister Gough Whitlam has been removed from office by Governor-General Sir John Kerr and replaced by Malcolm Fraser as caretaker Prime Minister. It's the culmination of a constitutional crisis the like of which the country has never seen before, one which will be known afterwards simply as the Dismissal.

An advert in *Time Out* gathers concerned Australians to a meeting in a pub where various left-wingers jump on tables and make speeches condemning Fraser and the Governor-General. A public demonstration is organised, and on a brisk, sunny November day Lindy joins the march on Fleet Street. It's unlike any demonstration she's ever been on. She's used to violence, arrests, police brutality. Here, a couple of hundred Australians march past Rupert Murdoch's building chanting 'Smash the capitalist press', then down the Strand, past Australia House, and all of it accompanied by just a small contingent of English bobbies. It is 'like sailing a boat on a windless lake', says Diana. They laugh at how easy it is.

In 1976 Lindy gets a job at a primary school in Swiss Cottage, teaching children to swim. One of the school parents is the conductor Sir Georg Solti, and when it comes to the summer holidays he and his wife ask Lindy to come with them as nanny to their two girls. They travel to a villa just south of Pisa in a large gated community set among pine trees. Lindy takes bike rides with the family along dirt tracks through the forest, and they all swim in the Mediterranean. One evening they invite the neighbour from the villa next door to come and play bridge with them all. The guest's wife, they explain to Lindy, doesn't play, so *she* will have to join them as his partner. The guest arrives, and he is Roger Moore.

Lindy, undaunted as ever, despite barely knowing how to play, rolls up her sleeves and does her best. He is charming and polite. 'Afterwards,' she says, 'Roger and I jumped in the pool and had a swim.'

And so, when Lindy finds herself back in London in 1982, as part of The Go-Betweens, it isn't her first time there, or her first time in Europe. The press don't ask her about it, but she has a past, a history. The two boys in the band have done almost nothing: she is all experience to their innocence. She has such a rich tale to tell, if anyone would ever think to ask her. From the moment she joins The Go-Betweens she is always with people younger than her, who have done and seen less of life. And instead of her greater experience being seen for what it is – an asset, a point of interest – it becomes something she seeks to conceal, because it gives away her age. She listens in interviews to the boys talking about music and films, and watches them being feted as intellectuals, while she is boxed into one of her two roles: Just The Drummer and The Woman In The Band. And occasionally she snaps and is then slapped down for being aggressive, and, really, from where I stand now, I'm surprised she didn't spend the whole of the '80s punching people.

I'LL BE YOUR MIRROR

Female friendship can be so complicated. Too often people are sentimental, and idealise it, focusing on the closeness, the warmth, the empathy. When I'm being honest, I will admit that I have hated female friends, possibly more than I have ever hated anyone else. Certainly more than I've hated any man. I wrote a lyric once about murdering my best friend and people asked me what on earth did I mean? I can't literally have murdered someone?

But it's a lyric about desire, a dream of what I wanted to do. And interesting to me is the fact that I wanted to murder the friend who got in the way, rather than the boy who ignored me. The feeling went so deep that it still flashed with a glistening fury when I fished it up to the surface of my mind some fifteen years later. Vivid and visceral, unspoken, unforgiven. As a feminist you are not supposed to compete with other women for the attention of men, but when I was young it was hard not to. Women are never as nice as we're often made out to be, and I was relieved when I saw this acknowledged by other writers. I wrote down two quotes in a notebook. This one, from Sylvia Plath: 'A woman, I fight all women for my men. My men. I am a woman, and there is no loyalty, even between mother and daughter'.

And this one from Fay Weldon: 'Fine citizens we make, fine sisters! Our loyalties are to men, not to each other.'

When I meet Lindy I've had no female friends for quite some time. As a teenager, I have got into the habit of valuing men and boys more. I'm not stupid; I can see that they have all the power, and all the fun. Until I rebel against it, I spend years wanting to listen to their music and read their books, to be in bands with them, just to be *with* them full stop. They are where the action is. They make the rules, and they can break them and get away with it.

I am careless about making friends with other girls; it's a habit I don't form. I make none at university, and then I live for a long time in the male world of the music business, with few female allies, surrounded by men in the studio and on the road. I become a bit like one of the Cool Girls described in *Gone Girl*.

And suddenly there is Lindy, who is unlike the English girls I have met, who is older than me, who talks and listens and shouts and smokes and shakes me out of my stupidity. As much as I'm drawn to her outrageousness and loudness, I'm drawn to her *positivity*. She is constantly upbeat, which is also in my nature. We are both full of a curious, almost gauche enthusiasm about the world. We are cheerer-uppers, bounce-backers, irrepressible, determined – me in a quiet way, her in a noisy way.

Within the world of The Go-Betweens she finds Robert and Grant endlessly depressing, describing them in an interview as 'the most boring and sad people . . . That's why they write the most boring and sad songs. They're moody and sad. That's our day-to-day existence and it comes out in our songs.'

She understands and appreciates the beauty that also comes out in the songs, but living and working with their introspection and angst is draining, exasperating, she thinks it is very self-indulgent boy behaviour. A woman wouldn't get away with it. A woman has to try harder socially. Has to placate, keep things running smoothly, not make unnecessary demands. There is no room for her bad moods, which will be called hormonal. Men experience existential despair while women have periods. Lindy and I both take the view that you can be existential some of the time, while also concentrating on having the time of your life. When The Smiths' *The Queen Is Dead* album comes out, Robert listens incessantly to 'I Know It's Over', and Lindy hears those dismal lyrics about soil falling over someone's head all day long until she is driven mad by it. In defiance, she puts on at full volume 'Shout to the Top' by The Style Council.

On the face of it there's nothing that surprising about our new friendship. Women are *supposed* to make friends with each other; it's taken for granted that we are better at friendship than men. We are more naturally empathetic and nurturing, motherly, better at sharing and caring for each other. But beyond all this is my suspicion that when women make friends, it is because we *need* each other more. We need allies. We look for safety in numbers. Someone to go to the loo with. Someone to say, 'Text me when you

114

get home'. Someone to look out for us on a boozy club night.

And we need our women friends in order to see ourselves mirrored and validated: to counter those moments we all experience when it feels like we don't exist in the world; when we look and can't find ourselves; when we are erased, pushed to the margins, written out of the story; when we start to feel invisible. In these moments, our female friends are invaluable to us. They reflect and embody us out there in the world; they remind us that we're real, that we're here, that we're not mad. Female friendship isn't a cosy thing: it's a necessity.

In a world like the music business, you need female friends not just to resemble you, but precisely to be different to you, to make the point that you are an individual artist, not just a female artist, as though you all speak with one voice. So it's just as important to me that Lindy is my opposite, as that she is my reflection.

When I meet her, I feel seen. I look up to her. She's older than me, and bolder, and so of *course* I look up to her. And although it seems to me that she is dominant, I think the feeling we have for each other is mutual. She reaches out to me. Her need is as great. We are both stranded.

With all this depth of feeling, it should be easy, I think, to write a song about her, but when I try, in 1987, I find that it's difficult. 'Blue Moon Rose' doesn't quite do her, or our friendship, justice, and it may simply be that without sex involved there is a lack of drama and passion, no internal tension to get a lyric really living, really breathing. It's clear that I love her, but there's a lack of specificity, a wrongness in the song's details. 'I have a friend and she comes from the high plains / Wise as the hills and fresh as the rains / Took me an atlas to find her town / And to realise that the world is round.'

I've no idea what I mean about her coming from 'the high plains'. I have succumbed to the temptation to fall back on rural imagery when describing an Australian, and it's ironic because, of course, Australia is very urbanised – even suburban in its large sprawling cities. I have a narrow idea of what her country is. She has lived a cultured life, full of politics and theatre and travels to Europe, but I paint her as if she's just blown in from Alice Springs.

Still, why *would* I have known much about Australia? In 1987, I'd never been there. To me, she represents Otherness. She has come from Elsewhere. In that sense, the inaccuracy is truthful. Much about her is mysterious to me, unknowable.

'I have a friend and she taught me daring / Threw back the windows and let the air in / She taught me how to be easy too / And I had a lot of unlearning to do.'

Those lines are a simplistic version of her, and of us. When I meet her, she does let the air in, but it proves much harder to teach me to be easy than I imply here. There's another line that didn't make it into the song, but sits crossed out in a notebook: 'She is older than me, yet she's restless and eager and wild / She's the best friend I had since I was a child.' And that is certainly true.

Better perhaps are the simple details of how we spend

time together, often in my kitchen, her wildness and my domesticity meeting in the middle and connecting with each other. 'I have a friend and we talk about books / She comes around and she drinks while I cook / She seems at home in this tiny place / But with her she brings wide open space.'

That still reminds me of those London evenings upstairs in my flat over a post office. A pan bubbling on the stove, a bottle of Stolichnaya fresh from the freezer sitting open on the table, her telling me something indiscreet, or imparting unexpected wisdom: 'Never make a big decision when you've got jet lag, Tracey. I mean it, take my advice, never do that.'

What I wish I'd captured in those lyrics is her inner electricity, the way it sparks and fizzes at me, the way it ignites me, how much I want to plug into it and use her as a source of energy.

On another evening, we are in her flat in Highbury Grange, and I am telling her about a moment when, as a teen, I'd feared that I was pregnant. Full of dread, longing for my period to start, I had also thought, 'Well, if I am, at least it would be *something*.' It was back in that time when I was desperate for anything to happen, to counter the aching dullness.

And Lindy narrows her eyes and says to me, 'Oh God, I didn't realise, Tracey Thorn, you're a *drama* queen under all that!'

She may have a point.

I think she is probably relieved.

*

By the mid-'80s, there is a gap between me and past friends, caused by my success, my ambition. Some make me feel like a sell-out, like I'm desperate to be a star. Lindy, while not so successful, is equally driven. She gets it. She is motivated, organised, and had wanted desperately to get out of Brisbane, out of Australia, which resonates with my equally urgent need to get out of suburbia. She isn't cynical about the idea of wanting to make it in the music biz. She knows and loves and hates the music scene as much as I do. We both belong and don't belong. We endlessly bitch about all the men – record company execs, other musicians. We are women of an academic bent in a non-academic world.

And for all that we share the feminist anger and frustration of having to deal with men in a man's world, we also share the simple fact of being heterosexual and being attracted to men. We understand the way we are both drawn to certain masculine traits: the hair on a man's forearm, the drag on a cigarette held between thumb and index finger, the rough jokes, the stubble in the morning, the unjustified confidence.

'God, I love Australian men,' I say to her one day.

I mean the ones I've met, who are all in bands and have a dark attraction to movies and drugs.

She raises both eyebrows. 'Oh, you haven't met any,' she says. 'These ones you know in London, they're not your typical Australian men.' She shakes her head. 'Not at all.'

But they aren't British men, that's for sure.

Slim-hipped, in belted black jeans with tucked-in black

shirts, they have a kind of cowboy swagger. The corners of their eyes permanently crinkled against a sun that doesn't shine here, they seem to be forever squinting towards a distant horizon, contemplating fate or anticipating trouble. They have gold teeth, instead of NHS fillings. Literate and articulate, they don't like the outdoors any more than I do. They carry books and hate the beach.

Lindy tells me that 'typical Australian men' are all shorts and thongs and tattoos and beers and unbridled sexism. But these Australian men drink gin and tonics, and speak in quiet clipped tones, and wander off to look at my bookshelves without asking, and tell witty anecdotes about Truman Capote, Billy Wilder, Frank and Ava. No wonder I like them.

Lindy isn't so sure. After she breaks up with Robert, she is forever falling in love, but usually *not* with Australian men. I note it all down in my diary.

I WOULDN'T HAVE ANY
FRIENDS

During the years of our friendship we often commu-
nicate by letter. She is travelling, or I am travelling,
and then she returns to Australia and our relationship
becomes long-distance. Each of us now has letters saved,
a random selection perhaps, hard to know how many are
missing, although she has many more letters from me than
I have from her. Either she saved them more carefully or,
and this strikes me as more likely to be the case, I wrote
more often.

As an archive, they are informal, mercurial, unreliable;
they bear cigarette burns, tea stains, smudged ink; they
carry the details of our lives on the fine tissue of air mail
paper, so fragile, so destructible. Often, they are undated.
We never thought we'd be reading them thirty years later
and would care about the details, so we merely write 'April'
or 'Monday the 15th'.

I don't always recognise myself now in the letters I
wrote to her; many seem camp and overblown, to be
straining for comic effect. I don't often talk about my
feelings or about anything difficult, whereas she is more
honest and down to earth. Her letters are more truly *her*

than mine are. I haven't yet found my voice. Where she is guileless and truthful, perhaps because she is older and has grown into herself, I'm still experimenting.

It was a time when we invented ourselves in diaries and letters. Not having social media didn't mean we were more authentic. My letters to Lindy are as stylised and performative as any Instagram account. I am often trying to be my Best Self, or what I think is my Best Self – witty and anecdotal, flippant and bitchy. I want never to be boring. It will be years before I dare to show a more vulnerable, fucked-up self to my friends, and in these letters any flashes of truth are often disguised as jokes.

For instance, I declare in one: 'I used to tell myself that dying wouldn't be so bad because I'd get to meet Billie Holiday and William Blake.' (Haha, death.) In another: 'We are on the cover of both the single and the LP, which is quite a departure for us and probably means we will sell no records at all once people see what we actually look like.' (Haha, failure.)

There is cruelty at the expense of others – 'Send photos of your tan and jokes at Grant McLennan's expense' – but then cruelty can often be a bond. Perhaps my bravado is partly that of the outsider. Lindy and I share a bitterness about the world we have found ourselves in, the dominance of the men who surround us, and whom we don't always respect. We also share the experience of trying to balance work and life, travel and love, excess and restraint.

This from her in 1986, written on two sheets of notepaper from the Diplomat Motor Inn, St Kilda, Melbourne, when she is travelling, and weary.

Dear Tracey,

This tour is pretty much like the other at Xmas except it's cooler (the temp). Feel very pedestrian a lot of the time and enjoy myself mostly when I'm on stage. We have an excellent crew and this is making a difference to our performance but the cities are the same, friends seem fewer and far between and our popularity only marginally increased . . . Tonight is our first night off in a week and naturally I can't sleep. We are in Canberra – the capital of Oz and a remarkably mundane town it is. Created as the head for government it is beautifully square.

We haven't reached Sydney yet – I should feel more then, I hope. Of course things have become quite complex now that Grant and Amanda are an item . . . I keep well out of it having embroiled myself stupidly at Xmas with others' problems and hope to pass the free time with old friends.

Lindy often veers between reckless disregard for her health and sudden new fitness regimes, this letter describing one of her many new resolutions: 'I've been looking after myself for a change, not smoking or drinking and I prefer myself when I'm not in the high pitch of hysteria I seem to reach so easily.' Perhaps in this instance being motivated by ill health all around her:

Rob hasn't been well at all and I think that has slowed us both down. I can't bear it for him when he's sick – bad back, flu, nose bleeds and it frightens me for myself as well . . . I went home as you know . . . My dad is very changed and his sickness is terrible. The whole family seem different, quieter, more adjusted and it is very hard to get used to. I feel clumsy and tactless around them because I haven't been there during the whole process. I don't know what to do . . .

I think of you and Ben and Peter often and wish I could write a more cheery letter. I was very sad your single didn't get as high as we all hoped it should have, but I expect the album sales will be compensatory in that regard.

Love Lindy

I reply in a style which will prove typical.

This is a gossipy first letter, the literary stuff will come later. Tonight we are going with S to see Citizen Kane and then probably he will get drunk and insult everyone. Which leads me to conclude that he is merely a Lindy Morrison substitute in our lives . . .

I am reading a good biography of Frances Farmer which I bought in America. It's by William Arnold and is called Shadowland, and it's a very serious journalistic-investigation type biography. He's obviously fascinated by her and appalled by the whole story. I think I might write to him . . .

Last night we saw Primal Scream and The Bodines (I have nearly found the perfect pair of white leather trousers). Bobby Gillespie wants to support us on our next tour. We start recording the new LP on March 10, working title is 'Shit Kicking Motherfuckers'. I think it suits us don't you?

I have enclosed a photo of Louise Brooks, to remind you what I don't look like . . .

Another from the same period is full of music gossip.

Apparently Roddy Frame (17) has disbanded the entire line-up of Aztec Camera . . . A world awaits further news . . . Geoff Travis heard Spring Rain on the Janice Long show the other night. Also, you are mentioned in T-Zers this week . . .

I must finish this somewhat rushed letter here and begin to prepare dinner for your long standing companion. I hope he has news of you, preferably illustrated with photographs.

It's mighty quiet here, no-one has spilled vodka on our floor since you left.

And another, in its throwaway remarks, is revealing on how lonely I can sometimes feel, dependent on the few people in my life I have become close to.

I have been hanging out with Marie Ryan, and Geoffrey Titley. In the evening Peter and Dinah came round for dinner, so as you can see, I have spoken to no one but Australians for days. This is an important point Lindy, if I hadn't met you I wouldn't have any friends!

Since then I've been alone. This is the first period of time I've spent alone in this flat, the first time Ben's been away. I've enjoyed the days a lot, but I don't like the nights much, I hate sleeping alone . . . celibacy isn't my strong point, however fashionable it may be . . .

I am reading the Collected Letters of Dylan Thomas . . .

Between the quips, and the celebrations of being drunk, which we often are – from Moscow, I send her a postcard: 'You would love it here, there are 47 different kinds of vodka' – a kind of longing emerges. Hidden in humour, as the truth so often is, I try to admit to her how much she means to me. Once unpicked and decoded, these jokes about booze – 'It's mighty quiet here, no-one has spilled vodka on our floor since you left . . . he is merely a Lindy Morrison substitute in our lives . . . if I hadn't met you I wouldn't have any friends!' – can be seen for what they are.

Declarations of love.

Although, as love so often is, my feelings are based on fundamental misconceptions.

The day we spend together at the Sanctuary looks like a simple scene, but when I think about it again now, I'm reminded how female friendships so often revolve around our bodies. We're supposed to bond over our shared periods, our breasts and blood, but just as often they get in the way and come between us. Shame and secrecy are as powerful as the urge to share. At my school, a girls' school, I concealed my periods and never spoke of them. I hid a tampon in a purse to go to the toilet, hoping it was invisible, and a friend picked it up and squeezed it in her hands. 'Hmm, what have we here?' she asked. 'A bullet?'

It might as well have been.

But Lindy, I imagine, doesn't have these inhibitions; she is not weighed down by all the burdens of shame and repression which have partly suffocated me up till now. She is a free spirit, at ease in her body, a natural woman. The scene is only simple because I have made the mistake of simplifying Lindy.

She was born this way. That's what I think. It's only when I start writing this book, and asking her more about her past, that I find out how wrong I've been.

I WISH I WAS PRETTY

Brisbane, 1956

She's not aware that there's anything wrong. She doesn't know this isn't what everyone sees. Clambering over the rocks on the riverbank, she has to watch her step, be careful not to slip, although she feels confident here, in her element. She loves the water, the way it reflects the light, the way it supports her weight. She's five years old, and is mostly left to her own devices. The two older sisters get all the grief – and dish it out too, constantly dobbing each other in, stirring up trouble. And the younger brother, the beloved son, he's the apple of everyone's eye. Whole new family now he's arrived. She doesn't mind. She's slipped into the gap between them and she's found her own niche. Down here on the rocks she can do whatever she wants, be whoever she wants, and up in her room it's all peace and quiet, playing with her dolls.

She loves her dolls, has more of them than any other girl she knows. They live in a cupboard on the verandah, and she brings them all out every night to sleep in her bed. It drives her sister Jenny nuts, this doll obsession, but who cares, they're her dolls, she can do what she likes. She holds them close and looks deeply into their faces, and it's good because she can really see these faces, close up like this. The grown-ups' faces, towering above her, are a bit of a blur. Well, everything is a bit of a blur; she looks at life through a sort of haze, and sometimes she's happy just to be alone in her bubble, with the dolls' faces near enough to make out. She assumes that what she sees is what everyone sees. The world out of focus, smudged like a ruined watercolour.

On the day she starts school there's a problem. The teacher keeps talking about the things that are written on the blackboard, and she can't make out what's written on the blackboard, can barely even see the board. She's going to have to tell someone. Then it's all interest and concern, now they're paying attention to her and it turns out there's something wrong. An optician, an eye test, and everyone is surprised to find out that she is extremely short-sighted. Her prescription is Minus 11, which is a lot apparently, and she's proud of this fact. That only lasts a short while, and then that feeling of being unique, of being a bit special, is ruined when they give her a pair of old-fashioned and unflattering glasses, with lenses like Coke bottles. They make her look stupid. She feels ugly and frumpy. Suddenly she can see her reflection clearly in the mirror for the first time, but it's awful. She doesn't want to see it. Now she's isolated in a new way, and she turns in on herself with self-loathing and self-pity.

No one really understands. Mum's too busy with the other kids, and always seems exhausted anyway. They don't understand each other. Everyone else loves Adelaide; she's fun and sociable with other people. But she's so strait-laced, so conventional, it drives a wedge between the two of them, especially as Lindy's childhood passes and she moves into her teens. Everything is strained. Maybe it's that Mum senses when her parental intervention would be a waste of time, but she often seems angry, and difficult, and there's an awkwardness, a tension.

Dad's OK but he's in his own world too. Lovable but sort of mad. Doc Morrison, he's a funny man, everyone says, and she thinks he is in both senses of the word. Funny haha and funny peculiar. He makes everyone laugh and tells a great story, but he too has his favourite things, his obsessions if you like. First, the boat. That's number one with him, he'd live on it if he could, and the river is the place he most likes to be. Second, a Broadway musical. Any one will do, he's seen them all; every time a show comes to town the whole Morrison family troop into Her Majesty's Theatre and settle down in a long row to see *My Fair Lady*, or *Bye Bye Birdie*, or *Gypsy*. And third, his new stereo record player. One day he makes the whole family gather round to sit down in front of the blessed thing. He's bought a vinyl record which plays the sound of a train, and the big deal is that you can listen to the engine noise going from one speaker to the other. And so there they all sit, cross-legged on the floor, listening to the train travel across the room, turning their heads like the crowd at a tennis match.

Between the two of them, Mum and Dad, they're fine as parents go, but they're not the kind you can confide in, about the way you feel inside, about how as the years go by you're starting to think about boys more than anything else, and about how desperate this makes you feel. Lindy hits thirteen and realises that boys are now everything to her, but she feels so plain that it makes her anxious. Her behaviour becomes desperate, aggressive even, as she pursues the unattainable. Tall now, and gawky, she develops crushes on the wrong people, on every boy she meets, has no filter or sense of judgement, exposes herself to ridicule. Above all, she has no concept, ever, of what it means to be sexy, of how it is done. Attracting boys seems like a magic trick that no one has taught her. She watches other girls fluffing their hair, tossing their heads, spraying perfume, and it all looks like arcane knowledge, some mysterious ritual that she has missed out on. Huh, she thinks, maybe it was taught that first day at school when I couldn't see the board. She's resentful.

One night, she goes to a dance with a boy, Robbie M., and they all go outside together, but he has only come outside to watch his friend with Lindy's friend. He doesn't even attempt to kiss her, just stands there looking at his watch and staring at the other couple, and all the time she's thinking to herself, 'So what is it that makes a person sexy? Is it just the shape of a body? Is that all sex is? And how do I learn how to play those games when I don't even want to and when I so desperately do?'

Who is there to talk to about all this? Nobody, that's who. Nobody except herself. She has a brilliant idea: she starts writing letters.

Dear Lindy,
You're 13 and this is 19 June 1965 and you have heard about people who write letters to themselves and on the 21st birthday open them. Well this is it.

Well, we'll start with home life. I really like Penny. She has started nursing five months ago and has grown up an awful lot. Jenny's skin was playing up but is now better. She can be awfully catty and rude at times. Ion is very mad sometimes. He has started playing with Clark Kent. I don't know why mum gets on my nerves sometimes. I think I'm something to blame and dad is still mad. I hate having our room not tidy at the moment and I always blame Jenny for not keeping it tidy. Paddy my cat is the darling. He had worms so we gave him pills. I hope he gets better.

Well, boys – I have gone through so many crushes that I'm nearly full of people. Boy I have a crush on Doug Stewart. He is so sweet and gorgeous. About six months ago he was playing up to me, putting his arm around me and trying to kiss me but I wouldn't let him. I went to Greg's party and he was there. We were mucking around with a tape recorder and he said into it, 'Lindy loves me Lindy loves me' and everyone heard and he asked me for a dance and I told him I wouldn't but we ended up dancing and I told him he was awful . . .

I have two wishes in life now – one to be very pretty, I am awful looking, and to be able to write.

Love Lindy

Dear Lindy,
This is the second letter you have written which you will read when you are 21. The date is 24 December and Christmas is tomorrow 1965. Life is very good . . .

Before I go I wish I was pretty, I wish Doug would like me very much, kiss me, he said he would take me out in two years . . . well. I also wish everything in this world would be fixed up . . . Also I am sure God is there now. Gail and I discussed.

Bye Lindy

Dear Lindy,

I am 14 now and I believe I have started to grow up . . . I wish I could meet someone who will like a girl with glasses!!!!!!! . . . I am now going through a period of I don't know what, I wish I could explain it. I think it's because of Jeff. So remember the big crush I had on Ian J that's over. I saw him again, he's married, he is nothing any more – me and my crushes. They tear me to pieces . . .

I love the world now but I'm scared of Jr I want to pass so badly, I am frightened I won't . . .

Penny is a beaut sister, I borrow her black stuff without her knowing and put it on my eyes to make me look better. Oh Jenny and I are all right, Ion is sweet but starting to get on my works, mum is difficult. Dad is sweet . . .

lots of love, Lindy

PS I wish I could pass Jr – I wish I could be pretty – I wish I could meet a nice boy. I think I am a bit selfish wishing for myself so, oh well, that's me Lindy.

The letters are ostensibly intended for her future self, but they read more like a desperate howl of confession. The words of someone who doesn't have anyone else to talk to, not in this way – brutal in their honesty, unsparing in their self-criticism. The unguarded quality makes you fear for her a little. So much vulnerability, so much openness. Is it safe to go out into the world like this, with a layer of skin missing?

She adores her teachers, loves them more than the other girls do, just as earlier she had loved her dolls more than other girls. Does she love everything more than others? Feel everything more deeply, or more acutely? Friends accuse her of sucking up to the teachers, but as far as she's concerned, they are all interesting and intelligent women, different to anyone she's ever met before: single women, some of them probably gay, the sports teacher definitely is. They seem inspirational. School is arranged in houses, and she is made senior captain of hers, Franklin House, voted by the other pupils, but is the first ever captain not to also be made prefect. The prefects are chosen by the teachers, and Lindy is not considered leadership material. She is boisterous, loud and enthusiastic, with no ability to censor herself. She says inappropriate things. Talks too loudly, laughs too loudly.

1966

Dear Lindy,

I'm 15 now and enjoying myself. Life is wonderful and I do love it. Junior is over and I think I have passed six subjects. I hope I do well, more than anything I want to beat Mags or at least come on tie. I don't want her to beat me, I know that's horrid but it's true. I don't seem to be able to get on as well as I'd like with my

133

friends. I lose my temper too often . . . I thought she was jealous of me but it was probably vice versa . . . I like all the teachers and I want to get to know them better because they are beaut. Miss Gill left and I was terribly sad. At the beginning of the year Miss Johnson came. I tried to become her pet and I nearly was. But I don't care and now I just want to be friendly. Mags etc said I was sucking . . .

Now finally on to boys. I have found I am not very popular with them. I think it is because I try too hard . . .

All my friends get on so well with boys I wish I could.

Must go,

lots of love Lindy

The glasses will be a torment for more than ten years, but at the age of sixteen she gets to throw them in the bin, becoming one of the first people in the country to have contact lenses. It's a turning point, liberating and trans-formative. Before and After photographs show the extent of the change. With the glasses – '50s Dame Edna-style winged affairs, the lenses so thick as to obscure her eyes – she is dimmed, hidden from view. Not plain so much as completely concealed. But without them she is revealed. It's like a scene from a corny old movie: the secretary removes her specs, and is suddenly all about sex – 'But, Miss Morrison, you're . . . you're . . . BEAUTIFUL!'

She shakes out her thick blonde hair, and we see her Hayley Mills snub nose, that wide grin, and eyes which are so frank and open they stop you in your tracks.

Dear Lindy, what an exciting time I have been having. Last night I was told by mother that I was boy mad, so it seems. I have been meeting new boys by the tons and getting crushes on them. Well to start with I'm completely over Doug Stuart since Easter. I think he's really revolting. He is so conceited and I wonder how I could have ever been in love with him. Easter he gave me a lift in his car from Surfers Paradise and he drove like a maniac. I slammed the door and got out and he called me back but I kept on walking. He really is pathetic. I was so mad with him because he had told me to walk behind him in Surfers. I had on my short minidress I love it but my legs are too fat to wear it now. I really am pleased I got him out of my mind.

A funny thing though, I'm wanting him to see me all dressed up with my contacts on and I hope people think I am pretty, as yet he has not seen me dressed up . . .

must go

Lindy

The bravery is dazzling. There's naivety, and childishness, and self-pity here too, but it takes courage to describe rejection and isolation. Such honesty in one so young. And the pathos of these observations, these pleas.

I think I'm something to blame . . . It's awful, I'm not pretty enough . . . I wish Doug would like me very much . . . I wish I could meet someone who will like a girl with glasses . . . I want to pass so badly, I am frightened I won't . . . I think I am a bit selfish wishing for myself . . . I don't want her to beat me, I know that's horrid but it's true . . . I don't seem to be able to get on as well as I'd like with my friends. I lose my temper too often . . . I thought she was jealous of me but it was probably vice versa . . . I am not very popular with them. I think it is because I try too hard . . . my legs are too fat . . .

She may have needed glasses, but she never had a problem seeing.

HELL, BUT I LOVE LIFE

But this isn't a cheerful, happy-go-lucky tale for her, this period of her life; there is real pain involved. Aside from all the rejection, or the imagined rejection, or the anticipated rejection, there are problems with her mother, which get worse as she gets older and starts having sex. Her mother finds out and is horrified. There's a boyfriend now, Peter, and he's handsome as anything, and this feels like a triumph to her.

1969

Dear Lindy,

It's been ages since I've last written but so much has happened. I don't know if I mentioned Peter in my last letter. Well Peter is the guy I like at the moment and he likes me . . . it started after candlelight dinner with Rob and Colin, we went swimming and after that I went into Peter's sister's room to change and Peter came in. We sat on the floor and talked and then he laid on the bed and I sat on it . . . I just put my head on his chest and said I was going to sleep. He started running his hand up and down my side and then told me to lie on my back which I did and then he started to kiss me. It was fantastic. He is the most fabulous kisser I have ever had so strong and masculine and when he was kissing me I couldn't believe it . . . He told me he loved me at Stratford Island for the first time on a hill in the wind overlooking the sea and moonshine. It was perfect. I said Peter tell me you like me . . . I like you, and he said Lindy I love you. He is so perfect looking, everything I love . . .

Hell, but I love life
lots of love Lindy

Peter is a clean-cut, good-looking young man of the '6os. He will go on to become a Qantas pilot. They drive out one evening in the car Lindy shares with her sister Jenny, and they are late getting back. Jenny, furious because her softball gear is in the boot, rings their parents, alarming them with the news that she thinks Lindy must have had a car crash – why else would she be so late home? This is pretty neat revenge, but not the most sisterly behaviour. Lindy arrives home to a torrent of anger. The car is to be taken away, and she is banned from the university dramatic society. Her dad gives a lecture which ends, 'a family is like a wheel, and if one cog slips out the wheel breaks so the cog must go back into place', which is a muddled image, but she gets the point. She is a part of something bigger than herself – a family – and can't act independently like this. Jenny has said, 'You know Lindy called Mum a bitch?' and now her parents are upset and crying, and they say, 'What is it, Lindy? What kind of girl are you? Don't you even love your parents?' and, feeling trapped by this, she shouts right back, 'No, I don't. I don't love you!' She refuses to burst into the tears they are expecting. Bites the inside of her cheek so as not to cry. Stares them out. Dad says she has no morals.

Peter writes a letter to her other sister, Penny, defending Lindy from the accusations:

Lindy rang me tonight and told me all this. She cried about it all morning. She is extremely sad and shocked that her family, that she loves, could turn against her . . . I think you should all be extremely happy that Lindy is your sister. She is incapable of intentionally hurting, she has a love and conscience as big as herself. Everybody has minor faults. Lindy has fewer than any I know. She is easily hurt . . . I respect her for her morals, I love her for herself. She is known at Uni to be the 'mad one' but also as 'Prudence'. She is 'mad' because she loves life.

Lindy's at the University of Queensland now, though still living at home, which probably isn't a good idea. She's meeting interesting people and getting new ideas, and Peter seems like he will be on her side through all this, but there's another letter from him to the sister, which is worrying and signals danger ahead.

Lindy will get into trouble with herself . . . Lindy doesn't have any aims except to find the secret behind the good-time people. Of course there is no secret. Lindy

139

is naive and can easily be led in search of the secret. Because of her trusting nature she will leave behind many of the good things in life, friends, and will regret it deeply afterwards.

This reads like a young man who is feeling threatened by the fact that his girlfriend has read a new book that has come out, called *The Female Eunuch*. She devours it not long after it's published and feels as if her eyes are opened, as if she can finally see clearly. Not the first time she's had that feeling. She is nineteen. The book makes her realise where she fits in, and leads to a drastic change of course when it comes to men. Almost overnight they become less important to her. She feels she has had no standards up until now, that she had been interested in any good-looking boy. She hadn't understood the difference between good, kind, sensitive boys and bad boys – they were all just BOYS.

Now she has had a revelation, and it is this: she doesn't need to get married. It's a momentous decision, and she feels strong and positive about it. It has chimed with something that's in her already. The book has simply put into words her instinctive feelings. Now she's on a brand new track, and sees the world unfurling in front of her, so many paths to choose, so much freedom, and then Peter dumps her, and she is broken.

He writes a letter to her, in 1972, outlining her new faults and expressing his dislike of her new style: the way she now seems to have courage and self-belief, the way she says FUCK, SHIT and HASSLE. He misses the 'tender

140

girl' she used to be. Says her new behaviour doesn't work for him. He's perhaps the first man to tell her that her personality – confident in herself, loud, opinionated, swearing – is terrifying to him, and that he is running away. But he won't be the last.

She tells me all this, years and years later, half laughing, half sad, reading out excerpts from letters, castigating herself, still trying to make sense of it all.

And I've still got all his letters – I mean, pathetic, it's pathetic. He found another girlfriend who was lovely, and so feminine. He said to me, 'You should be more feminine.' My father said to me, 'You've got to be more demure. You'll never get married unless you're demure.' But I used to hate when girls were coy, I really hated that. I always felt it was so dishonest, and I didn't wanna be dishonest.

I think how central this is to Lindy's character, to her essence. The hatred of dishonesty. The inability to play along with it. The bewilderment at how others can embrace it so wholeheartedly. Her devotion to the concept of the truth: an almost religious belief in it as the only way of being, and a revulsion at its opposite. This conviction will bring trouble in its wake, and make hefty demands on her life.

When I learn about the child and teen she used to be, they are not immediately recognisable to me as the Lindy I thought I knew. The uncertainty, the self-doubt, the miseries suffered over her appearance – they're at odds with my image of her. I had formed a first impression of her as a textbook heroine: a bold adventurer, no one's plaything, no one's victim. But I created that myself, out of almost nothing. Out of a glimpse, out of my own need.

By the time I met her, it was also an image she herself had worked at projecting. And she did it well. She was read as strong and assertive by all who met her. Only as I got to know her better would I see glimpses of this younger person, and these qualities which were never quite extinguished. An essentially romantic nature, a longing for love, an unswerving conviction that she wasn't conventionally attractive.

When I first saw her over my shoulder in the dressing-room mirror, I saw an outline, drawn in broad strokes. No details, no contradictions. This warrior, who seemed to be swooping in to save me, I was going to use her as armour. I would go into battle bearing her before me as a golden shield.

I wasn't wrong to think she was a heroine, but what I didn't know was what it had cost her to get to where she was, to be the person she was. And how her story was both the opposite of mine and also exactly the same.

When I think of it now, I ask myself, what does a mirror show us? Our image in reverse? Or our identical self reflecting back at us?

PART THREE

YOKO IS IN THE BAND

For a few years Lindy and Robert perform the intricate and awkward dance of being a couple in a band. They have records to make, interviews to conduct, gigs to perform – and a relationship to manage. Since they met, she has been something of a muse to Robert, and she is flattered, at least to start with. But it's unusual for a muse also to be a creative collaborator. Instead of being an external source of inspiration, she is in the way of the relationship between Robert and Grant. She is an irritant, and it's an awkward triangle, complicating her role. Songwriters and their inspirational girlfriends can often upset the dynamics of a band of boys, but this situation is different. In this case, Yoko is in the band.

Robert's songs become real once he meets Lindy, but are still more observation than passionate immersion. He writes about the impact she has had on him, how sexually stunned he has been:

> *Before we'd met, I hadn't wiped my feet*
> *Seen myself naked or . . .*
>
> 'Part Company'

A great reputation she kept up, my God! she kept me up.
'You've Never Lived'

I'd never met her type
She locked the door and the key
Opened the windows for the neighbours to see
Her climb on my knee

'Head Full of Steam'

But a muse is such a silent, passive thing, and that's not Lindy at all.

In 1979, at the dawn of their relationship, and before she has joined the band, Robert writes a defiant song called 'People Say', which sticks two fingers up at those who doubt his relationship with Lindy. It's an honest song in which he is defending her, but it's not *entirely* flattering to be told that everyone is advising your boyfriend to dump you.

'People say I'm mad to want you / People say I'm mad to need you,' he sings. 'People say I'm mad to love you, babe,' to which the only possible reply is, 'Well, thanks, I guess?'

A later verse is more unequivocal in its praise of her, declaring that even when it rains, 'you always stay dry / You've got your own private sun'.

Although even these lyrics prefigure another possible issue, they idealise Lindy, summoning up a person who can't be real. Songs often do this, poems too, putting the loved one on a pedestal or in a glass case, and looking at them from a distance. Robert detaches himself enough to write playfully about them breaking up, when they've only just got together. He sings, in 'Man O'Sand to Girl O'Sea', 'Feel so sure of our love / I'll write a song about us breaking up,' – and then goes on to do just that, in the song 'Part Company', describing their break-up years before it happens. 'And what will I miss? / Her cruelty, her unfaithfulness / Her fun, her love, her kiss.'

Maybe these lyrics *imagine* feeling something, rather than actually feeling it. They dramatise not engagement, but detachment. It's what writers do: analyse emotion, turn it into material. Everything is copy, as Nora Ephron said. Even love. Especially love.

In many ways their relationship subverts male/female roles; her forthrightness, her leading qualities, have enabled him to take the more submissive 'feminine' role. So she takes his virginity and washes his hair, while he puts on a dress and lipstick, and goes blond, perhaps partly wanting to BE Lindy, recognising her as some alternate version of himself. Aged fourteen, the first record he fell in love with had been Bowie's 'Starman', loving 'the voice pitched between male and female' – and at school he wrote a play about Oscar Wilde, while also dreaming of becoming a hairdresser. 'When I hold a hairdryer,' he writes, 'it's the only thing that feels as natural in my hands as a guitar.' He wears a dress on stage years before Evan Dando and Kurt Cobain, a decision which apparently fucks up the band's chances in the US.

So he is drawn to gender nonconformism, and presumably, at least at first, to these qualities in Lindy. But her assertiveness and her wildness, these things both attract him and eventually repel him. Terrify him even. His early lyrics portray her as an energy, a force to be reckoned with, but the book he writes years later is full of bitterness.

By 1986, their relationship is falling apart, and yet on the album they record, *Liberty Belle and the Black Diamond Express*, he writes three songs that are perhaps his most passionate lyrics about Lindy. In 'Head Full of Steam' he realises that 'to chase her' has been 'a fool's dream', and notes that, far from being his usual cool, calm self, he is now '104 degrees / With a head full of steam'. In 'Bow Down' he pleads with her never to slow down, and allows glimpses of an affair going wrong: 'You see things my memoirs just won't say . . .'

Amanda Brown joins the band at this stage, playing violin and oboe, and she recalls meeting the two of them: 'Lindy was really out of it on something – I don't know if she was drunk or . . . She and Robert used to take Rohypnols and drink. That was the first time I ever met any of them and I was really amazed by what an over-the-top personality Lindy is.'

The wheels are coming off their love affair, and there's a wild wilfulness to both of them. Robert tries to make it all sound romantic. In 'Twin Layers of Lightning' he describes them as 'Twin layers of trouble / Two times that might / Twin layers of lightning / Both of us can strike', and admits that if friends invite them round, 'Well, they're going to get a double act / We scream and we shout . . . Then we set a chair on fire / And we watch the whole house burn.' They are, he declares, in capital letters,

'TROUBLEMAKERS ON THE RUN', and their names are written in graffiti all around the town.

He talks about wanting to achieve either 'infamy or fame', directly quoting Lindy, who gave this answer when asked at the age of twelve what she wanted from life.

It sounds so glamorous, but then they have always been a spectacular, glamorous pair. Journalist and friend Marie Ryan describes them as 'both tall and striking. In my mind there was something of the New York alternative scene about them . . . Think Patti Smith and Robert Mapplethorpe. They just had that essence . . . Both being demanding individuals in their different ways, however, the relationship was doomed to fail eventually but ended up lasting around seven years. Lindy was never going to play a forever yin to Robert's yang and vice versa.'

The seeds of the trouble have been there from the start. Lindy remembers Robert saying to her that he wished she was seven years younger, and she remembers how much that hurt. She has lived with other people's scepticism, their outright disapproval. It seems that their relationship is always upsetting other people; they're constantly being told it won't last. It's Lindy's great fear – that ultimately it will not prove to be enough for Robert. She has been his first lover, and his first great love. He is still young, a minor star in a rock band, and at some point he will want and need to free himself and explore the world. She knows this, and she thinks it is only right. She has had a long history before him, and she has always believed in sexual liberation, so how can it be right for this man to have had only one lover? She thinks it is her duty to set him free.

It's hard to imagine a man feeling that about a woman, but there it is. She knows Robert will end up trapped and dissatisfied, and rather than let it get to that stage she forces a conclusion.

So she suggests that they ought to start sleeping with others. 'Start counting bodies / We'll both go half mad,' writes Robert. The recording of the *Liberty Belle* album is horrible, the two of them screaming at each other. 'A horrible couple to be around. We were explosive,' says Robert. 'It was dynamite in a bottle.' Yet that still manages to make it sound exciting, every row being proof that they are a big, loud, dramatic couple, a grand affair, a Burton and Taylor.

Lindy is fully aware that they are just bored with each other, bored and exhausted. Fighting at sound checks, disagreeing in public, in front of the group, trying hard to hang on to some dignity in the face of their collapse. Lindy tells her friend Kate that she wakes up to the fact that they are over long before Robert does. 'We were having sex one day,' she says, 'and he was playing with my clitoris. I looked up, and saw that he was watching the tennis on TV.'

The teenage romantic in Lindy has given way to a realist when it comes to matters of the heart. She is, after all, in her late thirties by now. And she's never quite bought into the notion of them as a perfect couple. In an early interview, they talk about how they have fights, and Robert says, 'We never go onstage angry at each other,' before being immediately contradicted by Lindy.

'I do,' she says.

If their break-up is partly her releasing Robert from his bonds, that doesn't mean there is no bitterness on her part about the fact that he very quickly hooks up with a new girlfriend. 'Before the bed was cold,' she remarks in a documentary, years later.

And she takes little pot shots at him after the break-up. In one interview, Robert is wearing 'a cream waistcoat and trews . . . the impression of the Victorian colonialist. "You've spilt something on your moleskins already," says Morrison, pointing to a hideous wet patch over Forster's groin area. "Is it a urine stain?"'

She tells the *NME* that even though she and Robert now live in separate flats in the same building, they meet on the stairs for 'glamorous fucks' and afterwards everyone is angry with her and says it isn't true, and she's angry with the journalist and says she was misquoted. Meanwhile I just think it's a great story, and in a letter to her I write:

Dear Lindy, I can't remember if I've written since the triumphant *NME* interview, so I probably haven't. Of course you came out the winner, hushing thousands of adolescent male *NME* readers into awed submission and wonder with your quote about the 'glamorous fucks'. You sounded like the kind of woman who would eat Tracey Thorn for breakfast.

Years later, in an Australian TV interview she will claim that she always knew they couldn't last. 'Our relationship never had a chance, because we were always in this

151

STUPID bloody band,' she says, and her voice rises until she is shouting by the end of the sentence, 'and it was never EVER gonna work, you know, and it's NOT FAIR!' Robert hangs on to the role of romantic, writing in a later song 'Dive for Your Memory', 'We stood that chance', and Lindy sees this as a tribute to their love, as a refusal to give up on what it meant. 'I'm gonna make you remember,' she says, 'that we had the most wonderful time, and we stood that chance.' That's what she believes he is saying.

But by the end of 1986, any chance they had has been consigned to history, and their separation, and the prickly relationship they live with afterwards, is another mile marker along the road towards the band's demise.

A BAD INFLUENCE

After Robert she is free again, and there are affairs with various men, and I start to notice that she is more vulnerable than I had realised. The realist who understood that she and Robert were bored, and took the necessary steps to end things, has now been replaced by a romantic who falls in love at every turn. I write in my diary, in May 1987, 'Lindy is in love and uncertain and miserable,' and it is unexpected to me. I've seen the bravery in her character, but not the sorrow, not the need, and as she embarks on episodes and adventures, she becomes surprising to me in her pursuit of love.

This particular man is unattainable, and it goes nowhere. Pretty soon he is replaced by another. When she doesn't return home to London from a tour in June of that year, I phone Robert Forster to see where she is, and he brings me up to date.

He said that during the European tour she was with Eric. When they reached Calais on the return journey, Lindy and Eric said a tearful goodbye, and the band went through passport control and customs towards

153

the boat. Suddenly Lindy burst into tears, ran back through customs, back through passports, caught up with Eric in the car park and they drove back together to Berlin, where she is going to stay for a week or so.

(Diary, Friday 12 June)

It's so romantic! A scene from a film. And none of this squares with who I had imagined her to be. We are still learning about each other. When she finally comes back to London, in between bouts of touring to support their new album *Tallulah*, we meet up to talk about love and the future.

Lindy talked about Eric and how in love she is, and how difficult it is because he lives in Berlin and on Friday she leaves for a tour of Australia and America and may not be back till October. They are talking of possibly getting married, and have to decide whether to live here or in Australia. I hope they choose here, of course. Lindy is really the only friend I miss when she is not around, because she is the only friend I talk to.

(Diary, Tuesday 30 June)

I am terrified that she will leave for good, and though I wish her happiness, I'm also selfish, and want her to fall in love with some English man, and stay in London, and always be here for me. So when this relationship breaks up, I wonder if I am as sympathetic as I might be, whether I am truly a supportive, understanding friend.

On Sunday Lindy got back from America and tonight she came round for dinner. She is looking great, very thin and hair very long. It was wonderful to see her again. She is exhausted from a long and gruelling tour – also she has split up with Eric, the man in Berlin.

(Diary, Tuesday 6 October)

She is wild during this period. It's clear to her now, looking back, that for a brief while she had become reckless and out of control. People had always called her those things, and now it's true. Astonished by her own disorder, she ricochets between men. And then suddenly, or so it seems to me, she becomes preoccupied with the thought of motherhood, and starts making plans, which this time involve a mutual friend.

Went with Lindy to the ICA to see a group called The Motorcycle Boy. Met Geoffrey Titley there – Lindy is still talking about wanting to have a baby, and tonight asked Geoffrey (who is gay) if he would be the father. They are great friends. His main reservation seems to be that he feels neither of them are in any financial position to support a child.

(Diary, Monday 19 October)

Like the love affairs, this doesn't come to anything, and by the end of 1987, The Go-Betweens have taken the joint decision to move back to Australia, it proving too difficult and expensive to carry on living in London and trying to make it as a band here.

She returns for a Christmas visit, and there is news of a new man – 'an American called Joe who plays bass in the band she is rehearsing with at the moment' (Diary, Tuesday 8 December). But the following year, this too has given way to new relationships.

> Went out for dinner. Wonderful to see Lindy again. We all drank champagne and gossiped loudly about everyone we know. Lindy is in love with John the head of an Australian indie label, but also having an affair with painter Robert Hunter.
>
> (Diary, Saturday 23 July, 1988)

More often apart than together now, we continue to write letters, keeping our friendship alive, sharing confidences about love and life, our hearts and our work. She travels more than I do, and The Go-Betweens are a much harder-working touring band, perhaps because they have to be. Struggling to achieve radio success and record sales, they fall back on the tried and tested way of trying to break through by playing live, and it is a gruelling circuit. The liaisons with men, which go nowhere, seem to emphasise the difference between our lives at this point. I am so settled, and she so rootless, and yet she is the older one. It's a topsy-turvy situation. In a letter, I tell her that Ben and I have just bought cats. 'You see how domestic we are becoming now you are not here to lead us astray. And I am no longer drinking since an unfortunate incident at a recent Smiths gig.'

We are both struggling within the music business, both

approaching a period when our love for it all starts to wane. I write to her.

> Our single came out about two weeks ago, showed its face to the charts at no 75 and then ran for cover . . . Ben says that pop music often seems to us like a frantic party to which we haven't been invited. I know what he means, and between you and me my application to Birkbeck College to do an MA is in the post. I hope all is well with you, write soon and let me know how many new boyfriends you have.

She replies from Darling Point, Sydney, on thin turquoise airmail paper.

> Dear Tracey, Honestly it is another time and planet in the Southern Hemisphere and I've been waiting for my mind and body to accommodate the changes but it is bloody hard . . . I arrived in Sydney, the days are endless, it's so bright until 9pm and for a while I simply sat in bars until 6am because it felt like it was only midnight. Lucky for me I've pulled myself out of that one – I was mixing with the criminal class, Robert told me, and I was going to get into TROUBLE.

Unlike me, she has nowhere permanent to live, although she has landed in luxury, staying at her brother's apartment on the twelfth floor overlooking Sydney harbour. She swims in the complex's pool and plays on her practice pads, but it isn't home, it isn't *her* home: 'I still haven't

157

found a place to live and altho' my brother doesn't mind, I do. He has a luxuriant life, and fine food and drink, but I can't relax. I feel like a freeloader amongst the affluence.'

I'm happy for her, and reply that:

I met Geoffrey just the other night and he said he left you very well and living comfortably in a nice part of town. I am very pleased and like to imagine you in luxury; foam baths and thick rugs and a good Hifi system . . .

But perhaps I haven't picked up the signals of how unsettled she feels.

Robert is the same, she says –

staying with the manager in a house with no letter box (it's bound to be a song) in Woolloomooloo, centre Sydney. We talk around each other about living together again (platonically) but then we run scared. We should give each other up

– and her family have been driving her mad.

Xmas was abortive because my mother told me in the kitchen between the cold turkey and plum pudding that the reason I was obsessed with trivial questions like sexism was that I had no real problems like family to think about. I skipped the plum pudding and left the next day. Now I feel guilty . . .

In a letter to another friend in 1988, she talks about her family gathering for the Australian Bi-Centennial celebrations and how awkward it is: 'I feel like an adolescent again. I was pretty well ostracised from the age of 21 and it's strange (inadequate word) to be part of a family again.'

Feeling misunderstood and cut off from our family is another thing we share. As a birthday present I give her an enormous hardback of the new Marilyn French novel, *Her Mother's Daughter*, a book in which women within the same family try and fail to understand each other, despite being inescapably bound together. Lindy writes to me:

> I'm gradually getting through it but it is a TOME and jumps from generation to generation willy nilly. It's so emotional because you keep reflecting on your own relationship and how inadequate it is and this makes me sad.

If only we could see each other more often, I think, we could talk about all this face to face, but the months of separation now make it all more difficult, and I can feel the sadness in some of the phrases of her letters. 'Write to me immediately please,' she ends one. 'I feel very cut off and long for some news of your doings. My love, Lindy.'

One day, she writes with an anecdote about Germaine Greer, knowing that I will understand and appreciate it, but there's also a revelation about dynamics within the band, and the increasing hostility she faces from Grant.

Dearest Tracey,

It's been pure wonder to get your chatty letters and I have a million things to tell you too . . .

. . . This is another story. Amanda tells me that the heroine Germaine is giving a lecture and would I like to go with Grant and her. On the afternoon of the event The Go-Bs are meeting to discuss the Capital record deal and as the meeting draws to a close they stand to leave. When I said I was going with Amanda to the Germaine lecture Grant jumps up and walks out alone in a real fit – I mean no disguised tantrum. Amanda then tells me that Grant has said she is not to see me (except in the band) and he does not want me at their flat. I am a BAD INFLUENCE . . .

Germaine was more than totally incredible. She is a great spirit. She tore at Oz nationalism to its core, she tore at the men, she was witty and beautiful. I got her autograph, 'To Lindy, my love Germaine Greer'. I was the first to ask and she looked into my eyes for a second. Bliss.

Feminism, love and art. The three themes that run through all our letters, all our conversations. This one ends, as so many do, on a note that is both flippant and serious all at once.

Rob F and I have been happily platonic. He is in love with the manager's sister (of bloody course) . . . I have seen three great films on video. Come Back to the 5 and Dime Jimmy Dean Jimmy Dean, Crimes of the Heart, and The Killing of Sister George. The latter is absolutely chilling. You must see them if you haven't already.

My love, Lindy. PS Every time you mention Geoff Travis my heart lets me know again: There's no one like him here, for sure.

After our *Idlewild* album comes out, which contains the song 'Blue Moon Rose', I write to her with an apology:

I will send you a cassette of the new LP – your name is misspelt on the sleeve, for which I apologise profusely – David Quantick reviewing the LP for NME assumed you had done all the drum machine tracks! I told him your thank you was just for being my best friend, not for being a drummer. I was interviewed last week on Woman's Hour on Radio 4 and they played Blue Moon Rose and we talked about how rare it is to hear a song about female friendship . . .

By the time anyone else hears the song, she is far away from me, and I miss her more than I can say. I think back to the Christmas of the previous year, when she was still in London and we had gone Christmas shopping together, then she'd come back to our flat to drink champagne, and we had eaten Christmas pudding with flaming brandy poured over it. I had played her 'Blue Moon Rose', without recording in my diary what she thought of it, and now I can't remember.

I had given her a Christmas present. A little silver brooch of a bounding jaguar.

BLAME THE GIRLFRIENDS

L ooking back, it seems like Lindy has always known
the band won't make it, like maybe she is the only
one who realises. Here they are on Australian pop show
Countdown around the time of 'Cattle and Cane', as early
as 1983, and they are poised on the brink of *something*,
excited, full of expectation. Lindy is in a brown leather
jacket with sheepskin collar, and she says, 'There's a buzz
– for a couple of weeks they talk about you and then they
forget about you. None of us care, we'll just continue
making our music whatever happens.' And then she goes
straight from this dismissive tone into a piece delivered
straight to camera. Smiling, breathy, eyes flicking up and
down, she says, 'Hello, I'm Lindy from The Go-Betweens
and you're about to watch "Cattle and Cane" on the
WONDERFUL programme *Countdown*.' On comes a video
of the band performing the song. They seem to be in a
barn, and Grant is wearing a kind of scarecrow's battered
trilby hat, with his hair pushed forward and looking like
straw. Afterwards, Lindy says of the performance, 'I'm
sure they put us in that set because of Grant's fucking
hat.' She knows they don't look like conventional pop stars,

knows that appearances like this won't turn a song into a hit.

'That is not a regular *Countdown* performance,' she says. 'That was not gonna make a difference, in my view.'

She is immune to the bullshit. She has more experience, more worldliness, more wisdom than the rest of the band. She suspects they are never going to become stars, or household names, or pop idols. She knows they are too odd. Meanwhile, everyone else gets caught up in flurry after flurry of potential, of *almost*, of getting close. Singles that sound like a dead cert, airplay that looks like it must lead to a hit. And when none of it works, and years roll by and there is no hit, and no increase in sales, everyone has a theory.

Someone says they don't make it 'cause they aren't good-looking enough. Lindy laughs as she says, 'The singles don't chart! I mean what a surprise! It must be the girls in the band! Grant said that to me. That was one of the reasons – 'cause there were girls in the band.'

Efforts are made to make the band fit a more commercial template. The emphasis shifts. Grant and Amanda make a pretty, straight couple, and so they become foregrounded. The balance of power has tilted. A band that began as an even-handed trio has become a five-piece, with a boy/girl couple at front and centre. The Go-Betweens begin to look like Grant and Amanda's backing band. Lindy is frustrated. Robert too. She knows the record company wants them to be more than a cult, but she's convinced it won't work, and doesn't know why anyone bothers.

In many ways it's been great for Lindy since Amanda

joined the band. She has an ally, a mirror image within the group. And she no longer has to be Everywoman. She tells the Australian music paper *RAM*, 'I was sick of being perceived as some symbol of womanhood, which is something I couldn't possibly sustain. I can't possibly represent all women, yet I was being more and more expected to do so . . . by outsiders, who really seemed to expect I'd be "the woman" of this band.'

Not having to represent *all* women is a relief. Having two women means that they can each be distinct from each other. Just as Grant and Robert are defined in opposition to each other – made sharp by their differences, their contrasts – so it is for Lindy now that Amanda is in the band. They don't cancel each other out, but in fact throw each other into sharp relief, into singularity. Each can be an individual.

And yet even in their individuality, there is an inevitable bond, a fund of shared experience, which is nourishing to Lindy, reduces that feeling she always gets from Grant and Robert that she is somehow *too much*, that her experiences are *weird*. She tells the *Melody Maker*, 'I can say to her that I'm expecting my period and she'll UNDERSTAND. Men are so hard. They expect so much from you. And you must never show your feelings. I get so TIRED. The particular three boys we work with are emotionally controlled and stable – they don't REACT.'

Even so, when a Brisbane newspaper prints a photo of the band, they caption Amanda as Lindy, and vice versa. From the outside, these two women are sometimes interchangeable.

And Amanda is told from the moment she joins the band that she is not to write songs. That job is taken.

Both Lindy and Amanda, at different times, bear the weight of being the 'girlfriends'. There are never two couples at once in The Go-Betweens; they're not quite ABBA in that respect. But still, they are a band of high romantic drama and sexual tension. Lindy and Robert's break-up will contribute ultimately to the break-up of the band, and that break-up will end Grant and Amanda. Either way, it isn't safe sleeping with the drummer, falling in love with the songwriter.

And the antagonism between Grant and Lindy, which has been there from the beginning, gets worse as time goes by, and Amanda finds herself in the middle. It's another fault line. In 1988, Lindy writes a letter to her friend Joe in which she describes how toxic the atmosphere can be, Grant having told Amanda that:

> he disliked me, I was a bad influence. I'm surprised how badly I've taken this. It is really quite stupid of him but it's ghastly to think I'm working in such a vicious circle. Robert was little help – I suppose he'd known all these years . . . In my mind I'm preparing to get out, it's about time.

When the frustration about their career hits its peak, Robert and Grant both fall into the trap of thinking that a greater focus on the two of them might be the solution. It's so tempting to look for easy answers. When the single 'Streets of Your Town' gets on to the A list at Radio 1 and still fails to crack the Top 75, it is deemed to be the fault of the record company, who haven't worked the track hard enough.

And Lindy is aware that the two women in the band are also vulnerable when it comes to looking for somewhere to place the blame. She says in an interview, 'I've often noticed in all-boys' bands that it's always the girlfriends that seem to give the bands the problems. And when there's a scapegoat needed, it's always the girlfriends.'

I AM JUST A WRECK

Lindy lives through all the years of trying to make it: the producers and the A&R men; the drum machines and the reworked singles; the makeovers and the videos; and the touring, the endless touring, with all that it entails. It leaves behind a residue, an actual paper trail of evidence, an archive of written material. Here, for instance, in a designer's office, gathered together during the making of a compilation, are boxes and boxes of – what – clues? Treasure? Sifting through it all, like a detective, like an archaeologist, feels like an act of discovery and recovery. But also like opening someone's mail. Looking for a story, and making excuses about the intrusion involved.

The curating of all this material is both ordered and random, careful and careless at the same time. It was one of the jobs a band's manager used to do, and reminds me how much of a physical presence we used to create in the world. Look at the paperiness of it all. Here are copies of old *NME*s, ragged and dog-eared; cuttings in scrapbooks, snipped out and glued in, years and years ago; press releases and tour dates; old reviews; forgotten interviews. All of it on paper, more paper, and still more paper.

Here is a box full of tour itineraries which, like diaries, tell the story of a hard-working band. There's no way to put a positive spin on the life they summon up, no glamour to be found here. Each page bears the details of the slog: that day's hotel, the hours of travel, the location of the gig, the capacity of the venue, the sound check time, the onstage time. Who is sharing a room with whom.

There's a trip to the US in 1985, where in New York the band are playing at Danceteria, and staying at the Iroquois Hotel, 49 West 44th St: 'one suite, four beds'. The tour winds up at Club Lingerie in LA, where they sleep at the Hollywood Celebrity Hotel on Orchid Avenue: 'two doubles and one cot', after which they return to New York to play CBGB. The accounts record quotidian details like immigration fees, two days per diems ($120), van rental and a drum kit for the CBGB show.

Days and days on the road, spilling over into months and years.

Here is a 1986 Australian tour itinerary, with four gigs in Sydney, five in Perth, three in Melbourne, and then more in Noosa Heads, Byron Bay, Canberra, Bunbury, Geelong and Adelaide. Handwritten notes scrawled in the margins detailing interviews and phoners, all in Lindy's handwriting.

Here is an itinerary for a European tour, May 1986. Seventeen gigs, with 'more dates to follow'.

Here is a tour from 1987 – with nine dates in California alone.

If you read between the lines, you can discern a lack of career progress, evidenced by the unchanging venues.

On the *Liberty Belle* UK tour, they are playing at the

Town & Country Club in London, and small clubs else-where: the Escape Club, Zhivago's, Rooftops, the Hoochie Coochie, the Bierkeller. A year or so later, on the *Tallulah* tour in 1987, it's still the Town & Country in London, and still the Hoochie Coochie, and still the Bierkeller. After five years of touring the UK it remains a gruelling schedule. The pages stink of hard work. There's supposed to be an arc of progress, but quite often there isn't.

The piles of paper build up, towers made from the remnants of the past, the story of this band who were friends of mine, and whose lives I briefly shared, whose dreams and disappointments I heard about, and under-stood. Come and see, look, here it all is.

A flyer for a gig in 1985 at the Boston Club in Tufnell Park, with Raymonde and Discobolisk.

A press release from Beggars Banquet in 1987, after gossip that they were splitting up: 'The band would like to reassure their fans that they're more together than ever.'

A pair of Hoverspeed tickets, Dover to Calais.

Pages of tour expenses all handwritten, because 'my typewriter is broken'.

A note about visas being refused.

A note about a Double Taxation Agreement for Italy.

A slip of paper which records a trip to A&E for a band member on tour, one of the usual on-the-road complaints, a chest infection, a temperature.

A handwritten letter, on blue notepaper, from the Tudor Court Hotel, which includes a bill for non-appearance. 'Your party never turned up, we have received no cancel-lation either by phone or letter. I refused rooms for the

weekend because they were already booked to you . . .
Yours faithfully L. Howells (manageress).' Attached is an
invoice – 'i nights B and B £85.50, and for breakfasts, an
additional – £17.50'.

And here are four more letters from disgruntled tour
managers, promoters and gig bookers. They are over thirty
years old, yet the bitterness they describe feels fresh and
furious. It begins to occur to me that I shouldn't be seeing
these at all, but it's too late now. Anyway I can't resist. I
think of Lindy, reading letters she wasn't supposed to read,
and I nod in recognition.

And I read on. Phrases leap off the page, their anger
undimmed by the years:

> looking for recompense – unfinished business – gullible
> of me – I trusted you – the miserable pittance received
> – you certainly saved money – uncaring judgmental
> company – risible wages – personal conflict – debacle
> – extremely disappointed – I had no idea how difficult
> – lack of comprehension – what are the band's inten-
> tions with regard to this debt? – I have resigned from
> this tour, I am just a wreck – I will not be part of the
> music industry any longer.

Reference is made in one letter to a band member being
'tired' after birthday celebrations; another compares the
difficulty of booking their tour to 'the invasion of
Normandy'.

There is sarcasm, disappointment and disgust in these
letters. It is shocking, but also, from this distance of time,

quite funny. I can't be sure what the rows were about. Money, it mostly seems. Poor communication, misunderstandings, false expectations. The classic story of a band on a shoestring, forgetting that those around them are not engaged in the pursuit of fame and just want to be paid. Not listening to advice that contradicts what they want to hear. Not always being on their best behaviour.

At the top of the ladder of success, when the money comes in piles too high to measure, and you've lost count of your limos, and you're drowning in drugs, and have a temperature-controlled wardrobe for your fur coats, you can sing about imagining no possessions. Down here in the gutter, someone has to pay for breakfast, and sort out that visa, and wait in A&E, and all for a pittance that makes them want to walk away from the music industry for ever.

WHAT ELSE IS NEW?

The band's final album is *16 Lovers Lane*. It is their last attempt to make a breakthrough pop record, and it founders on two separate rocks: first, that they are never going to be that kind of band, and second, that by now they have all had enough of each other.

A documentary series called *Great Australian Albums* focuses on this one, and opens by outlining all the complex relationships within the band – Robert and Lindy, Grant and Amanda, Robert and Grant, Lindy and Amanda – until Lindy butts in, shouting, 'How many times can we talk about the fucking relationships in the band, man!' Even talking about it afterwards will become boring.

The album producer, Mark Wallis, begins by recording Grant and Robert playing the songs as a duo, thus excluding Lindy. At the same time, her dad is very ill, dying in fact, and so she is absent for much of the recording. Drum machines replace her, and when she's able to, she comes in and overdubs snares and cymbals and brushes and percussion. Still, she tries, as far as is possible, to hang on to what has always been rhythmically interesting about them – her refusal to conform. There's a song called

'Clouds', which has a three and a half-bar verse, and so is considered too unconventional to be a single. People are infuriating, she says: 'they always want things to be square, all in blocks of FOUR!' She mimes square blocks with her hands, exasperated at listeners and their staid requirements.

Lindy is on her own now, in liking their funny-shaped songs. In the studio, the producer, and bass player John Willsteed sit, head in hands, going, 'She can't play, she can't play,' and it is impossible for a band to continue in that mood. It seems to have been accepted that Robert's arty songs are not going to be the route to success, and so Grant's more regular pop/rock tracks become the singles.

Lindy's father dies midway through the recording, and after it's all over she writes me a letter, detailing what a horrible time it has been.

1 June 1988

Dearest Tracey,

I had been waiting until I could at least write you a cheerful letter with lots of good news but time keeps passing and nothing changes very much so I'll press on regardless. The LP is finished – I missed all the mixing because of my Dad's death – it's been horrible losing him and I'm still abstracted – not nearly as bad as my Mum and sisters I think. It's today I felt a change. I gave up smoking (both sorts of which I was doing heaps) and saw a doctor – I'm not very healthy but at last I feel motivation to improve.

She notes that the 'LP is untitled as yet altho' "love is geography" is a good contender.' The line her dad had said to her, all those years ago. And she is kind about the songs and the players, even the ones who have been unkind to her. 'It's a very acoustic album,' she says, 'sounds like the acoustic demos but our new bass player being a fine musician (guitar as well) has provided some beautiful lines.'

With her usual positive spirit, she ends on a note of optimism — 'We put on a huge show with magicians on Sat night at a theatre and we were very successful I think. Perhaps we will do something in this country after all' — but I can't quite tell who she's trying to convince here. Me? Or herself?

One of the strangest things about this final record is its cover, which consists of three individual photos of Lindy, Grant and John. The new bass player, who never really liked the band, and the two members who have always hated each other. And like some *GQ* cover shoot, the two men are fully clothed, while Lindy is naked beneath a bolt of silk which is wrapped around her body. The end of the cloth stretches away out of shot, held by an unseen hand. She looks up and away to her right, a rare instance of her not making eye contact with the camera, as if she has already half checked out.

The band once again tour extensively with the album and, in their biggest live moment yet, bag a support slot with REM in Australia, New Zealand, the States and then Europe. The touring is relentless, and needs to make money, as they are still selling no records and still having no hits. When it is all finished, they end up back in Sydney, still no further on, back on their arses.

And at this point everything begins to unravel. No one knows what direction they should go in. Robert and Grant are writing acoustic, singer-songwriter type songs. Lindy and Amanda are beginning to talk about starting their own band.

She writes to me about hanging out with a lot of her old friends, taking solace in the company of people who inhabit another world: 'It's wonderful that they are not in the music business and we seem to have settled into our old selves together.'

Her love life is as eventful as ever.

I had the most wonderful boyfriend for a month – he runs an Oz record company . . . I adore the guy but naturally ended up scaring him off by my emotional/sexual/time demands. He says he's busy but he hasn't been in touch for a couple of weeks except to tell me he would call tonight which I'm still waiting on. I've had a terrible broken heart over this. I really have fallen head over. But then what else is new.

LEAVE HIM

1989

Finally – finally! – it all comes to a head, and Robert and Grant, both desperate to escape, decide that they will break up the band in the most brutally symbolic manner possible. They arrange that on the day after Boxing Day each of them will confront their lover, or ex-lover, and sack them. At the exact same moment, but in separate locations, Robert will sack Lindy, and Grant will sack Amanda. The thinking is hard to fathom, impenetrable even. The weird symmetry; the ex-couple and the current couple; the men telling the women; the brutal display of where the power lies. There is a glaring absence of band democracy, any sense that this could be a discussion in which all voices might be heard. The act itself seems designed to humiliate and to hurt. A childish, unnecessarily theatrical scheme, it is no wonder that it ends in catastrophe.

The hour arrives, the news is delivered, like a telephoned warning of a planted bomb. And the explosion is immediate. The two women, in separate rooms, in separate houses, can't see each other, which seems deliberate. Like blindfolded hostages, they are powerless. Lindy catches a glimpse of her reflection in the window, but she has to imagine Amanda's face. She wonders if it is as desolate, as furious, as her own.

Robert describes Lindy's reaction in these terms: 'Her bitter laugh almost held a touch of admiration. How had two guys she'd always regarded as being weak-kneed suddenly found the balls to do something like this? . . . Lindy walked to the phone. She looked back at me after dialling and then turned in profile to talk. Her first words: "Leave him."'

For Lindy, on hearing the shocking news, has immediately called Amanda, asking whether she has just been handed the same information. She has, and her response echoes Lindy's. She is packing her stuff and leaving Grant, and as she says now, 'Listen, I didn't need telling.' Indeed, she is resentful of any suggestion that it was Lindy who dictated her reaction.

What did Robert and Grant expect to happen? If your boyfriend chucks you out of the band, do you automatically leave him? My answer is an authoritative and resounding YES. It is an act which, in its abandonment of trust and its forceful reminder of who is in charge, would kill love stone dead.

When Robert describes the scene he realises, way too late, *years* too late that 'of course Lindy and Amanda would feel betrayed and angry after the years of work and emotional energy they had put into the band', although this is a weak half-apology more than a true recognition. And it is still blind to the sheer self-destructive folly of that betrayal.

Robert and Grant had realised early on that as a simple

duo – two boys together singing their songs – they were not a sparkling enough prospect, so they decided to add a girl. *Bang*, they were a more interesting group. But in that moment they got more than they bargained for; they got not a pliant, gamine, striped T-shirted pretty French *fille*, not a librarian, not a Karen, or a Lee Remick or a Clark sister – or all the other imaginary women.

They got Lindy Morrison.

Only a year before the symbolic sacking, at that Sydney TV interview in 1988, Lindy had still been looking at Robert with real affection, but now, on Boxing Day 1989, everything has fallen as far as it's possible to fall, and in this flippant moment of dismissal it feels as though Lindy has never been truly understood or appreciated.

Both of the women are furious, and disgusted, everything is over, and Amanda walks out on Grant, and Lindy walks out into the rest of her life.

DON'T THINK I'M MAD

Lindy's feelings about motherhood, like most other things, have always been extreme. As a young woman she is certain she doesn't want children. Many young women feel the same, but not so many take the decision she does in 1979, which is to get herself sterilised. She is absolutely sure about this, makes an appointment at the clinic, is determined to go through with it. Then the night before the trip to hospital she reads an interview with Bette Davis. And Bette Davis says that having a child was the best thing she had ever done in her life.

Lindy sits up with a start, and her mouth drops open, and her mind is changed. For a woman – a heroine! A goddess! – like Bette Davis to say this about motherhood makes Lindy see it in a whole new light. From that moment on she knows that she *does* want a child, and after the split with Robert it becomes an ever more insistent urge. By 1989, when The Go-Betweens are at their end, she is determined to have a baby.

With no man on the scene, she toys for a while with the idea of going it alone, of getting pregnant and becoming a single mother. But in October 1989, still a few months before the band split, she writes to me about a difficult decision she has made. She'd been sure she was the kind of woman who could do this alone, but suddenly and unexpectedly the reality has hit her, and she wavers, deciding instead to try and settle down with the man she is currently seeing. The letter she writes is full of honesty, and an admission of sudden fear.

Dearest Tracey,

. . . The psychological change that occurred in me after I returned here, saw my family, came to Sydney, saw John, can only be described as very bleak. I'm not sure I can talk about it now but I felt I was on this terrifying rollercoaster and I wanted off. I was scared without John (and perhaps you and Geoffrey) and when I saw John here I couldn't face being without him. His offers of a future together made sense. The hardest thing for me was facing that I wasn't the strong independent person I hoped for (needing a man so clearly) . . .

Meanwhile I've been going to the gym and working out every day. Aerobics, stretch, nautilus weights. I'm obsessional. After quitting smoking (everything) I've gone up a size so I'm converting to muscle. I look good.

. . . I have to go as I have an eye test in town. Write back soon. I miss you very much – don't think I'm mad . . .

Love Lindy

I hope this isn't all too strange.

Of course I don't think she's mad, or that this is particularly strange; I'm in awe, as usual, of her frankness, her willingness to be open about her own vulnerability, even as she weaves her way through another challenging set of circumstances and decisions. I simply haven't appreciated her longing for a baby, for a settled family life. I have been in danger of imprisoning her in my own narrow perspective, fixing her for ever in my mind as the free one, the independent spirit, never a wife, never a mother. In this moment, what I suddenly realise is that our roles have reversed. The mirror has switched us around.

While she is dreaming of motherhood and domesticity, I am on tour, and for once enjoying it. This time, I am the one who is out there in the world, free and adventurous, breezing along the highway, wind in my hair.

5 July 1990

Dear Lindy,

. . . We did the whole tour by bus, no planes at all, so this meant lots of overnight drives straight after gigs, and I kept thinking how much I enjoyed this life on the move, always leaving towns and thinking ahead to the next one. The longest drive was 1200 miles from Boulder to Sacramento, which took about 20 hours, and we woke up to see the sun coming up over the desert, and then just desert and more desert for hours. I read Evelyn Waugh all the way, gazing out at scorching salt flats, and then turning back to read about England's lost honour, and chilly morning mists, and thwarted Catholicism . . .

Pretty soon, Lindy is pregnant, and sends me photos of herself with a huge belly, joking and larking about, her smile bigger than I have ever seen it. In 1991, her daughter Lucinda is born, and she forms a band, Cleopatra Wong, with fellow ex-Go-Between, Amanda Brown. For both of them, this is a fresh start. 'I had come out of The Go-Betweens at the age of forty,' says Lindy, 'with a child, and owning nothing but a drum kit.'

And then Amanda is pregnant too, and the two of them continue to experience what it's like being 'women in a band'. A piece from a music paper in 1992 reads: 'Cleopatra Wong's record label rooArt apparently not all that impressed upon discovering that singer Amanda Brown is pregnant, sex symbols heavy with child being a tad hard to market.'

Lindy and I stay in touch, but it becomes more intermittent. I'm still working hard, recording and touring, although we've hit a few career ups and downs now, and in 1992 Ben falls ill and our career stalls. I write her a long letter about what has happened, which is full of pain and honesty, and more open than I had been in the past.

Although, as usual, I can't resist one funny line. Two friends have just got married, and, as I describe it, 'She wore black and had a panic attack but otherwise I believe it went well.'

The following year, she writes to tell me what her life is like now.

Dear Tracey,

I've just reread your letter from Aug, and it's such a great description of your life. I think it's great that you have set up the EBTG headquarters at home. It's really interesting the type of people and things you discover about the music industry when you look after yourself. And it sounds like you're getting around as well. You actually make me homesick for London. I wish I could be at the Hampstead gig . . .

Now Lucinda is 2, I only get 3 working days a week, when she goes to childcare. It's really full on with Lucinda. She follows me from room to room saying, 'what you doing Mama' and the moment I pick up a drumstick, it's 'My turn now.' It's all happening so fast. I actually got clucky again now Lucinda is not a baby. No, I won't have another child. I've just stopped being tired. Anyway she is a beautiful person, my daughter, with an extremely good sense of humour, I just wish I could teach her to use the potty.

Still haven't decided on a direction musically, I saw this percussion group the other day, they were pretty good and I might ask their leader if I can play with them. For the last 6 months all I've done is play the snare drum at home and I like the sounds and accents you can get out of just one drum and two hands.

I'm actually employed to look after an intellectually disabled band at the moment. It's a great job, they are all really fun and quite competent. I play drums with them as well and they use all the stock show biz clichés, it's hilarious . . . I always go on about this I know but I would like to get over there to see Beggars Banquet. They still won't admit the Gobs are gone and my debt to them is growing every time Rob and Grant do another loser album . . .

I miss Rob a lot, but so much has passed it's impossible to make contact. I'm happy you see Geoff Travis. Give him a big kiss for me . . . I still smoke pot when Lucinda is not around, it makes me quite eccentric I think.

Got to go now, hope we can get together sooner or later, I will get over there eventually. Miss you both and love to Ben,

Love,

Lindy

Cleopatra Wong only last a couple of years, and Lindy never really returns to life as a full-time member of a band. She has different ideas now about making music. She's been worn out by the mainstream music business, and left disillusioned, so she starts working in community music, spending a lot of years with the Junction House Band, the group she mentioned in her letter. She describes them in an interview: 'The lead singer is a fabulous song writer. He is autistic and has written a song called "They can't do this to me". It deals with the subject of people making fun of others. It never actually mentions disability but it deals with all of the issues. Every time he does that song he ends up screaming, lying in the foetal position on the floor. Now that's what I like to see. The expression coming out through the musical performance.'

She says that there can often be a lot of yelling, but then, she is used to this. 'I've been working with professional musicians for 25 years and we yell at each other.' She's good at this work, because, as she puts it herself, 'I'm tolerant and accommodating . . . and I'm not interested in making my own art work. I've had that career. I don't want to be a pop star.'

She's beginning to wake up to the truth about how little money she earned from all those years in The Go-Betweens, and is shocked to find that she actually made more cash in just three years with Cleopatra Wong. 'I've been exhausted by the rock industry,' she says in another interview. 'I want to relax, and settle down a bit'.

She becomes an advocate, helping others to get hold of their share of royalty payments; she gives lectures on copyright issues, on contracts and rights; she attends conferences where she speaks as an expert, an industry insider. And all this is personal too. She spends many years embroiled in heated exchanges with the former Go-Betweens and their record label and management for money she believes she is owed.

A postcard arrives in October 1994 announcing: 'Will be in London for one week, end October to 5 Nov. Bob and Rob F and Grant are finally settling the money!! I'm staying at Geoff Titley's. I'm praying you'll be in town and able to see me. Love Lindy.'

She has made her move into a new world, and she is living a new life – when, suddenly, the old one rears its head.

*

Robert and Grant – who have each continued for a while as solo artists, making albums and touring, neither with a great degree of success – have decided to reform The Go-Betweens.

In 1996, French magazine *Les Inrockuptibles* is preparing a front-cover multi-page spread on the band, which will tell their story and include a cover-mounted CD to introduce them to new fans, thus securing their place in rock history. The paper offers to fly Robert and Grant to Paris to play a show. Robert explains that they can't do this as the original line-up of the band, but suggests the two of them perform with new musicians, still calling themselves The Go-Betweens. This is the moment when the new incarnation of the band is born. Robert will write later that they were using 'a name Grant and I, while acknowledging all who had played in the band before, felt entitled to'.

When the magazine appears, on the cover is a photo from the period when the band made *Liberty Belle and the Black Diamond Express*. The headline reads: 'Is this the most underrated group in the history of rock?' Both the photo, and the group they are talking about, includes Lindy. She is both in and out of this group; she both is, and is not, part of the story. The telling of it is being taken on by others, and she is in danger of disappearing.

She is disappointed by all this, but remains diplomatic, at least in public. In an ABC documentary about Australian music, *Long Way to the Top*, where she is one of the main commentators, alongside Nick Cave, she says that the new incarnation tarnishes the completeness of a body of work made by a unified band. She had played on all six of the band's albums before the split-up, and for her, that is the complete Go-Betweens work.

In private, she is less diplomatic, and so am I.

I write to her in 1997, by email now, with the subject title 'Go-Betweens?'

Hi Lindy,

How are ya? A few weeks have lapsed already since our last mails but I have been spurred on to write by the appearance this last week of the 'Go-Betweens'. They played at the Fleadh in Finsbury Park on Saturday and then on Monday night at the Forum. Ben and I went with Geoff T and it was a very nostalgic night, happy mixed with sad, good with bad. There is a girl bass player and a boy drummer (wrong way round), Robert and Grant still enacting the exact same roles – Robert hilarious, sincere and camp all at once, Grant still too serious, watching Robert (who never looks back at him) . . .

We did of course consider boycotting the whole affair, possibly even demonstrating outside with 'No Lindy, No Go-Betweens' banners, but in the end curiosity won out . . . So that's my Go-Betweens report, thought you might be interested.

Weird without you though, not really real . . .

All love

Tracey xxx

To which she replies:

I can hardly pretend I am happy about the Gobs but I can imagine from your letter that the songs would have stood the test of time and that makes me happy. But I have to admit to an indiscretion – I rang Bob (the manager) the other night and Beggars (the label) and told them if I see my face in another Gobs reunion photo I WILL MEET THE BOYS AT THE AIRPORT WITH A RIFLE. Gee they took a long time to laugh.

As usual though, the best bit of her email is to do with her personal life. She has been having an affair with a married man, which is fizzling out, and she writes:

He is such a weird guy, so straight and so bent or are all married men like that? . . .

I fucked my best friend the other night . . . a beautiful man, I always loved him. Well, to quote Michael Stipe, I said too much, I didn't say enough, and baby do I regret it . . . I am such a dope with men.

I was sitting on his cock working out our lives together. Can you believe it.

I can believe it, Lindy, yeah.

After all these years, I'm finally getting the measure of you, and if only we lived nearer I think we could have had an even closer friendship now, moving through the years of success and failure and motherhood and love and work and ageing, sharing so many thoughts and experiences and unspoken things.

Instead of which, because of the great distance involved,

and other less forgivable things like tiredness and distraction, we start to drift apart from each other, and the bond loosens. When in January 1998 my twins are born, I write her a brief letter enclosing pictures of the girls: tiny, huge-eyed, doll-like. It is the last actual letter she has from me. As we open it now together, in 2019, the photos fall out from the envelope, where they have sat all these years. Our lives have moved on similar tracks but a very long way apart. In this last letter to her I say:

I really hope you do come to London this summer because of course I want you to see them, and we can sit and compare baby pics, and be generally Mumsy, and who would've thought we'd all turn out like this eh?

And then the line between us goes quiet.
Twenty years slip by.

PART FOUR

GOOD GIRL

The year I turn fifty-seven I find myself in a crisis. It is partly, though not entirely, centred on my marriage, which goes through a bad patch. Not the first one, true, but perhaps the worst. A thirty-eight-year-old relationship, however successful, can contain within it pockets of toxicity: unresolved issues, personal baggage, mutual grievances. Some of this stuff is black as tar, and as hard to remove.

I feel myself coming adrift, unsure of what I want, unmoored from where I am. The timing coincides with the last of the kids being about to leave home: a typical hinge point of life, one of those moments when you have to redefine yourself, decide what's going to happen next, who you want to be.

It isn't a midlife crisis – I've had that already, about ten years ago. And it isn't the menopause – I've been through that too, and even then I hated having my every existential thought connected to my periods. As Clare Dederer writes in *Love and Trouble*:

the very term annoyed us. When men have existential crises – when Richard Ford, for instance, limns the male at midlife – it doesn't get called by some dumb hormonal name. It's a "universal human experience". We were having those, "universal human experiences", not menopause, or so we kept telling ourselves. Women can, after all, see the same thing on the horizon that men see.

Yes, I can see something on the horizon, a potential narrowing and then an inevitable ending, and it's not as far away as it used to be. But more than that, I'm not sure how I want to get there, how I want to spend the time leading towards it.

This crisis of identity is like a whirlpool, into which my marriage gets sucked. It is explosive and destabilising. We both end up feeling angry and stuck. There are conversations not being had, and the ones we do have end in shouting and recriminations, neither of us quite saying what we mean, neither of us quite being heard. I storm out of the house more than once. Hotel rooms, minibars, dance floors – all get more of my business than usual. I sit in a taxi drinking gin from a can and thinking hateful thoughts. I walk and walk, and then stand and stare at the river, its bridges and beaches, the pull of its tide, and the buildings that tower above. I consider getting a tattoo that says FUCK YOU and I think the YOU is everyone, or possibly even myself, and I've no real idea why I feel this way.

I read and re-read Deborah Levy's *The Cost of Living*, written about her divorce. She describes her marriage as a boat, feeling herself to have been tossed overboard into the sea, and unsure whether or not she wants to swim back to it. I wonder whether I feel the same. But then, she asks, what is the point of a life without love, without risk? It is, she concludes, 'a waste of time'.

I confide in various friends, but with a certain blankness, a detachment in my telling. I rant and rave, but without shedding a tear. I become repetitive. I talk and talk, and then afterwards can't remember a word I've said. I know I'm in a bad way, but I find that I'm unable to cry. I think I'd feel better if I could cry, so I put on records that usually move me. Rickie Lee Jones' *Pirates* album has never failed me before, but this time it does. I play 'We Belong Together' and I play 'Living It Up', and I sit stony-faced, dry-eyed and staring at the wall, and it frightens me. What shall I do with all this pain if I can't even find it?

I start questioning how relationships work, how they can survive so long. When I find a diary from 1988 I realise I have thought about these things for a long time. This is what I wrote, thirty years ago, and once again, Lindy is part of it.

Monday, 4 January 1988

I'm reading Simone de Beauvoir's *The Prime of Life*, the second part of her autobiography, which Lindy gave me. It's very interesting to read about her relationship with Sartre – at one point she says that they decided to sign a two-year lease:

'I could arrange to live in Paris during these two years, and we would spend them in the closest possible intimacy. Afterwards, Sartre suggested, I ought to take a job abroad too. We would live apart for two or three

195

years, and then rejoin one another somewhere – Athens, maybe – where we could, for a longer or shorter period, live more or less together. We could never become strangers to one another, and neither would appeal for the other's help in vain; nothing would prevail against this alliance of ours. But it must not be allowed to degenerate into mere duty or habit; we had at all costs to preserve it from decay of this sort.'

Is that what I had wanted for myself? Could it have worked? It's a fantasy, isn't it? A crazy dream, a mad idea of how love can be, almost certainly impossible. Definitely idealistic, and romantic in its own way. But did I *want* to try? I don't remember.

I feel a strong need for solitude and independence, a reaction to the child-rearing years. All that self-sacrifice, all that self-effacement. The children have been at the centre of my life, but who, or what, should it be now?

I feel claustrophobic, and at the same time I have lost the ability to compromise. I am less malleable. My clay has set hard, and I have become more myself, or a new version of myself, one with sharper edges. But I don't like these feelings, and I fear that indulging them will lead only to loneliness. Is the choice between being lonely or annoyed? Do I want comfort or excitement? The uncertainty churns, until all I am aware of is an unspecified rage.

I talk to other women friends who report feeling the same. Now that we are no longer just mothers, who are we? What is our role? Who needs us now? And what do WE need? Or want?

I keep noting down quotes that speak to me.

From Agnès Varda: 'In all women there is something in revolt that is not expressed.'

From Anita Brookner: 'I feel quite deeply, I think. If I am not very careful, I shall grow into the most awful old battle-axe.'

The uncertainty feels like it is connected with my age, and yet reminds me more than anything of my adolescence and young adulthood. It is like an uncomfortable return to youth, with all of its vexing questions about how to become a person, a whole person, the person you most want to be. Or the person you *have* to be.

I turn these thoughts upon myself, cursing my indecision, my passivity. I read Kim Addonizio's poem 'Good Girl', and I think it is talking about me.

Look at you, sitting there being good.
After two years you're still dying for a cigarette.
And not drinking on weekdays, who thought that one up?
. . .
don't you want to mess it all up, to roll around
like a dog in his flower beds? Aren't you a dog anyway,
always groveling for love and begging to be petted?

Late at night, when I've had drinks, I feel loose and like my wheels are coming off, and I'm not sure if it's a good or a bad thing. I go out in the evening, dressed up, talking, getting drunk, dancing, feeling a bit wild and young, feeling alive. I miss euphoria, and am euphoric when I find it again. I have to ration myself, and not do it too often. It's an escape, not a solution.

I see planes overhead and I want to get on them.

In the midst of feeling like this, I book a flight to Australia. What better test of our boat than to swim away from it as far as possible and see if it pulls me back.

A LIABILITY

Revisiting a friend after a long absence can be a scary thing. It begins to occur to me that I've embarked on both a project – to tell the story of Lindy, and of our friendship – and a long journey – to reunite with her in person – without any clear sense of the likely outcome. And now my mind is all worry, all questions. Will I still know her after all this time? Will she still know me? Will I still *like* her? What will happen if I find I don't? If too much time has passed, we are too different, have drifted too far apart? It's been so long since we were close. We have been useless at keeping in touch, and although we have started talking again via Skype, the conversations have been quite stilted and formal. I have a sinking feeling that I'm not sure who she is any more, and that it is a big ask to be writing a book about someone I no longer know.

When I land in Sydney at 5 a.m., it's pouring with rain. I've travelled for over twenty-four hours into the same landscape, the same weather. By 10 a.m. I'm in a cab heading over to Lindy's flat, near Clovelly Beach in the eastern suburbs. I climb the stairs to the second floor where she is waiting for me at her open door. I haven't seen her for twenty-five years, and she leads me inside and I'm waiting for her to say 'Hello' or 'How was your flight?' or 'OH MY GOD, it's been so long!' but instead she says, 'So, Tracey, do you want this skirt? I'm throwing it away, it makes me look fat, but do you want to try it on? You can have it.'

She is holding out a knee-length skirt with a gathered waist.

I say the first thing that comes into my head, which happens to be the truth. 'I think it will make me look fat too.'

She looks closely at me. 'Yeah, you've filled out a bit.'

My dungarees, which I have worn for comfort, for a day spent kneeling on the floor sifting through boxes and files, suddenly seem wrong. I should have made more of an effort. There is a pause.

'Right,' she says, 'we should get started with these letters. That's the first thing we have to do. Come on.'

I had forgotten this basic fact: with Lindy, there is no preamble, no small talk, no social niceties. She cuts straight to what interests her, brushing aside anything else with a wave of her hand.

'Could I possibly have a glass of water?' I ask.

I am five hours off a flight from London. Being back in her company, after a gap of a quarter of a century, while in the grip of extreme jet lag, is a near-hallucinogenic experience.

After making me a cup of tea, she whisks me into her office, where I note the stack of Marilyn Monroe books on her shelf. *Goddess*, *The Marilyn Handbook*, *My Week with*

Marilyn, My Sister Marilyn, Marilyn: Norma Jeane by Gloria
Steinem, *Marilyn in Manhattan, Marilyn Monroe: The Final
Years*, Monroe's *My Story, Before Marilyn, Dressing Marilyn,
Marilyn at Twentieth Century Fox, The Marilyn Encyclopedia*.
This was something we shared, this love of the old screen
goddesses: Marilyn, Bette Davis, Frances Farmer. I'd
forgotten. We used to talk about them, about their
glamour, and their strength of character. They were an
escape for us, from the world we'd found ourselves in,
which had so few roles for women, and which were all
so limited, so dull, so drab. For a brief period I had dyed
my hair blonde and toyed with emulating that elusive,
golden quality that coalesced around these stars, and
around Lindy.

Her flat is filled with the sound of ticking, which comes
from a number of clocks on the walls, all of them out of
sync with each other. A pendulum swings from one,
wooden and ornately carved, like a cuckoo clock without
the cuckoo. On the hour, it chimes – BONG BONG
BONG – startling me each time, and I wonder, 'How can
she live with this? How can she *sleep* through this?'

As I'm wondering, she catches my eye and grins.

'Isn't it great?' she says, and I nod dazedly.

It's like being in the workshop of an eccentric watch-
maker.

The flat is designed for life in a hot country: hard stone
floors, no rugs, no radiators. But outside the rain beats
down on the pavement, on the rooftops, drowning the
bougainvillea on her balcony. We're in Australia, under
English weather. In the middle of the room are a couple

201

of large boxes, and from one she pulls out a folder. It's full of letters from me, dating mostly from the '80s. She has kept all my letters, stored them in a folder, in a box. I find this intensely moving.

But Lindy isn't in the mood for sentiment; she has a plan for the day, and it involves me making a copy of every one of these letters.

'It's important. You have to do this right. You'll kick yourself if you don't do it right. For the sake of completeness, you need to scan them all.'

This isn't what I had planned to do. I would rather sort the letters first, prioritise the important ones and just scan those. As I start to read through the pages it's clear that some of them are simply boring – filled with stories about holidays, news about our cats. I want to focus on the more interesting ones, and not waste time.

I am also very tired.

But she is adamant, and immovable, and I wonder why I am surprised. She has always been like this. I had imagined that today would be emotional in many ways. And yet here we are, half an hour into our reunion, having what can only be described as a row. A polite row, but nonetheless.

Lindy won't concede her point. And nor will I.

We have both become stubborn, a little set in our ways. Two old biddies, we are each determined to be in charge.

I start scanning some letters, while she sits at the computer facing away from me. Here is the solution, I think, and so while her back is turned, I slip any uninteresting letters back into the folder, and scan only the ones I want.

202

The morning passes in this manner.

I think we are both happy.

There is a week of this – intense days and nights which have to stand in for missing years, conversations in which we try to knit our friendship back together, picking up dropped stitches, mending holes. After the first session with the letters, we begin to relax, and by the third day in each other's company we have our own private jokes, which cause us to lock eyes and giggle in company.

Round at a friend's house, Lindy insists on putting on her Spotify playlist, at full volume.

'I can't stand background music,' she says. 'If we're going to listen to music we should listen properly. It should be too loud to talk.'

We're drinking afternoon gin and tonics, and nobody feels like disagreeing with her, so up goes the volume, and on comes Barbra Streisand singing 'He Touched Me'. Lindy sings along. Then Stella Donnelly's 'Tricks', followed by The Waterboys' 'The Whole of the Moon'. When Sia's 'Chandelier' starts up, Lindy and I join in, straining for the high notes. We're a bit drunk by now, and I touch her arm and call her darling, and I think, 'Oh, look at us, camping it up, ramping up the closeness. I remember this feeling.'

The next song is Lorde's 'Liability' and Lindy crosses the room to turn it up even louder. There is no going back now. I know we both love this one, we have talked about it before, but it suddenly strikes me how much of herself she must see in the lyrics. How often has she felt, or been told, that she is too much for people? That they pull back from her, sometimes make other plans, think that she's a liability? It's one of those lyrics, proud and vulnerable at the same time, which allows you to revel in being the thing you're accused of. I feel wounded on her behalf, when I think of all the times she has been thwarted and belittled and undermined, and at the same time I feel as admiring as I ever was. Who wouldn't want, at least some of the time, to be thought of as a liability?

We have only a week, to make up for twenty-five years, and I had been afraid I wouldn't like her. Instead, the opposite is happening. I am remembering the history we have, how hilarious she is, the sheer fucking buzz of being in her company.

In a Mexican restaurant in Brisbane we sit, over frozen margaritas and nachos, to a soundtrack of The Human League, Pet Shop Boys and Talk Talk, discussing secrets and sex. She has a new lover, and we talk about the years, sixteen of them, since she last had a man. She tells me that she lost interest during her menopause, when each hot flush came with a catastrophic sense of impending doom, a craziness like nothing she had felt before – not the madness of youth or the wildness of her twenties, but something new entirely. And, having had breast cancer, she couldn't take HRT, and so just had to tough it out.

The cancer had come just after her sister had died from the same disease.

'Sheer terror,' she says. 'I just assumed I was going to die.'

A lumpectomy and radiation left her with one rock-hard breast which she became sensitive about.

All of this – the breast, the menopause, motherhood, and also just getting older, feeling more set in her ways, more stubborn, more unable to compromise – meant that for a while she eschewed men. There were chances, often for one-night stands with younger men, but she couldn't be bothered, and she thought this was for ever.

And breaking free of men was a relief, she says, the escape from that constant falling in love with everyone she slept with.

'I'd spent my life circling men,' she tells me. 'And finally I realised I could be effective without them. Falling in love all the time had *disabled* me.'

Now she is in full possession of her senses, and in full control.

Her current, and unexpected, affair, is making her happy because she is *not* madly in love with him. She has moved on, and this feels like progress. The only drawback is all the body maintenance that's required once you're in a new relationship.

She asks her daughter where people go nowadays to get waxed.

'No one waxes any more, Mum,' replies Lucinda scornfully, 'they get lasered.'

She is aghast at the effort of it all. All the trouble that women go to, how it's just taken for granted.

'Although there is one bonus,' she says of her new lover, 'he goes down on me, and it's fabulous! No other men have done that for me.'

'Really?' I say. I'm astonished. She has always been my icon of sexual liberation, so I assume she does everything, all the time.

She thinks for a minute, and then says, 'Well, maybe it's me, maybe I've got a terrible cunt,' and we *scream*, and I fall over sideways on the bench.

At her brother Ion's flat, we are discussing the fact that he had to hide being gay when he was young, as it was still illegal in Queensland. Someone asks Lindy, 'Did you know he was gay?' and she is affronted.

'Of course I knew,' she screams. 'Of course I did!'

She turns, and addresses the whole room: 'I think I'm being underestimated here. Don't underestimate me.'

A minute later, she loses it again when someone refers to us as girls rather than women.

I'm not sure whether the apparent anger is real or feigned.

But then I'm not sure about a lot of aspects of her personality. As much as she is irreverent and unpredictable and fun, she is also touchy, alert to the possibility of insult. I am reminded not to patronise or undermine her. When she hires a car in Brisbane, and promptly loses the key in a café, I attempt to console her.

'Don't worry,' I say, 'anyone could have done it. You have a lot of things to remember.'

'No, I don't,' she snaps. 'Don't talk to me like one of your daughters.'

Walking down the street, we find we need directions, and she calls out 'Hey!' to a guy delivering mail. Then, striding towards him, calls 'Hey!' again. He stops in his tracks and shakes his head, so offended by this manner of address that he refuses us any help. Lindy simply turns and walks away, assuming that he is in a bad mood. She even *forgives* this bad mood.

'It's a hot day,' she says. 'He's just taking out his frustration on me.'

I am about to say that perhaps it is she who has been rude to him, but I swallow it back down.

A few nights earlier, she had shouted out 'Mate! Mate!' to a waiter, who had brought her a gin and tonic, instead of just a *gin*, as she'd requested. He had been equally unimpressed, and she had been equally impervious.

And now there is a slight jockeying for power between us. Good-humoured, but still there. In Brisbane, her home town, she refuses to admit any difficulty in knowing her way around. But the city has changed, and she loses her bearings. Meanwhile, being a stranger, I have the map open on my phone, so I'm the one saying, 'Oh, it's left here,' or 'No, we just need to go over this junction and then turn right.'

She's not happy with this.

She looks at me a little suspiciously and says, 'I thought you'd be more helpless,' and I wonder if she would have preferred me to be.

I'm the younger one, and the tourist here, so am I meant to be in second place? Am I breaking the rules of seniority? I remember how much she likes to be in charge. At her apartment building, she is head of the residents' group, and because of this, allows herself to store her drum kit in the cleaner's cupboard. She also has an informal tennis group, and has been in charge of this for many years. As her brother Ion says, who on earth is going to put their name forward to challenge her?

We are in Brisbane because she is speaking on a panel at the Big Sound Festival. During the discussion she is asked a question from the floor about how to survive in a small town, how to create cultural spaces outside a metropolitan area.

Lindy replies, without hesitating, 'Oh no, you can't, you just have to move to a big city. You have to leave the small town. In fact, you have to leave Australia. It's too small, it's no good for you.'

There is uneasy laughter from the audience, and the moderator seizes the microphone from Lindy, who has gone considerably off-message.

'Haha, or perhaps,' she says, 'you need to find like minds, start an open mic night, start putting on gigs, stuff like that.'

Lindy looks chastened, and she takes the mic back and apologises for being discouraging.

Once again, she has said the wrong thing.

Once again, I find myself delighted by her irreverent honesty, her inability to toe the line, to ever be boring.

But she is a minor star here, recognised by the waiter in the restaurant, who is one of her former copyright law students. She is loved and admired, has status, and I'm proud to be her friend. I feel like showing off our old connection.

We arrive at a drinks party, to which I'm not, technically, invited. She announces herself – 'I'm Lindy Morrison' – and her name is found on the guest list. The hostess turns to me, questioningly, and all I can think of to say is, 'Um, I'm *with* Lindy Morrison.'

And that does the trick.

The city is full of people in town for the conference, so she keeps being recognised.

She has assured me that so far she has kept my book idea a secret. 'I haven't mentioned it to anyone yet,' she says, 'because it's all so uncertain.'

The first person we bump into says, 'Oh, I hear you're writing a book about Lindy! That's so great.'

I look at her but she evades my glance.

The second time it happens she is, once again, apparently oblivious.

After the third or fourth time, I realise that she has in fact told *everyone* I am writing a book about her. She seems completely unabashed by the discrepancy.

We drive over the Go Between Bridge and I take a picture of her at the wheel.

We go to see the house in which she grew up, looking at it from the opposite bank of the Brisbane River. The river is wide, and fast-flowing. I had pictured a creek. And I remember her telling me that she would row across here, in a little boat, on her own, from the age of about five.

That girl, half blind, determinedly wielding her oars on the choppy water. She is still that girl. There is a youngness about her that looks like innocence, but isn't, that looks like naivety, but isn't. It's a cousin of these things: a kind of openness to the world? Wonder?

Everywhere we go we are told to quieten down. During the speeches at the Big Sound party she is shushed, but responds by pulling me closer and talking ever so slightly louder. At an outdoor restaurant at Clovelly Beach she laughs so loud that other people turn round to look, and she apologises, but they say, no, it's good to hear someone laugh. We talk about a description of her in an interview which focused on this laugh of hers. 'Lindy Morrison,' writes the journalist, 'has a laugh that could bring down buildings. It goes until she can barely breathe, thus forcing her to make a sound like a donkey as she desperately inhales at the end of the hysteria . . . AH-HA ha ha ha ha ha ha ha ha ha ha, hee-haw!' She'd been upset about it at the time, and I say that it's typical male cruelty in a description of a woman. It was intended to humiliate you, to draw attention to something about you that was considered aberrant, unfeminine. It was a policing of your behaviour. And she nods gratefully.

She stands up, and pulls on her denim jacket and turns away from me. On the back of her customised jacket, rhinestones in cursive writing spell out the name 'Morrison'.

We discuss books, the way we always did.
   . . . *I have a friend and we talk about books* . . .
   She tells me she's been reading an essay about cultural appropriation. This particular writer, who is white, has been hauled over the coals for writing a black character, but Lindy says she's on the side of the writer, who has

asked: what does it mean for fiction if we can only write ourselves? We're left with only the option of non-fiction.

I'm not so sure. I think this writer is a repeat contro-versialist, and I fear that she's joined the ranks of those who say things just to get attention.

'I think I understand why people get fed up with writers describing characters who are not them,' I say. 'I mean, look at us – we're always complaining about how men write women. It drives us mad. We feel appropriated, misunderstood, misdescribed.'

'Yeah, that's true,' she concedes.

'And I remember what I was like at university. I was all about cancelling the canon – down with Dead White Males! That was back in 1983. It's what the young always do. Burn down the older generation! Stop thinking you know everything.'

She's looking at me.

'Maybe all any of us are saying is: don't just assume you know enough to write this character. Listen more. Pay more attention. *Write better*, for God's sake. Maybe that's the side we should be on.'

She pauses, and stares at me, like I've made an unex-pectedly interesting point. Screws her eyes up at me slightly.

And we both smile.

It's a familiar pattern to our conversations. I end up not certain that we agree, but it doesn't much matter. We enjoy the disagreeing.

And, of course, I tell her that Ben and I have been having troubles. She's sympathetic, but unsurprised. It's a mystery to her how any relationships last. She also jumps to conclusions.

'So, is one of you having an affair?' she asks bluntly.

'No, no, nothing like that,' I say. 'It's just long-term relationship stuff, how to carry on living with someone after a long time. We've both changed. Or maybe it's more that we're both *changing*. We're in one of those periods of transition. Shaking off the past without being sure yet what the future is. Or what we want it to be.'

Other friends have nodded gently at this point in similar conversations, and offered kind words or recognition.

Lindy says, 'Well, you know what I think. It's what I've always thought. Marriage is a prison. I shouldn't really say this, but I'm never surprised when men leave their wives. They just can't possibly cope with monogamy.'

I blink at her, wondering whether this is helpful.

'It's impossible, staying with someone your whole life. You can't *live* with another person,' she says. 'Not for a long time.'

'Well, *you* can't,' I reply.

She wrinkles her nose, and grins. 'It's true,' she says. 'I can't.'

And she looks at me, her face asking, 'And what about you? Can *you*?'

She is sixty-seven years old now, but still hasn't bowed down, slowed down. Her Facebook page is a catalogue of always being out, always busy, always looking like she's having fun. Here is a photo of her backstage with Australian band Rolling Blackouts Coastal Fever, and she's standing in the middle of the five of them, posed like a team leader, like a mascot. Here is a video of her playing drums on a verandah, and she's in a skirt and trainers, throwing out the same chaotic energy as ever. Here are her photos from a Laibach gig in Sydney, and here is the list of influential albums she has chosen: Lou Reed's *Transformer*, *Hunky Dory*, Otis Redding, Judy Garland, Barbra, Sinatra, *Tapestry*, of course, and *A Journey Into Stereo Sound*, the one her dad played, with a photo of a train on the cover. Here is a photo of herself from the mid-'80s in NYC, standing next to Tom Waits, who is waving at the camera. Here are some links to songs by Courtney Barnett and Billie Eilish.

And here is another link, to a film of herself with young Australian musician and songwriter Alex the Astronaut, who she works with in 2018. In the video, the two of them sit and watch that Sydney TV interview from 1988. Lindy thinks it is twenty years ago, and has to correct herself that it's THIRTY years ago. 'Seven years before I was born,' says Alex, to which Lindy replies, 'Oh, I can't bear it. Kill me.' Together they watch the Lindy from back then, explaining how her parents would have preferred her to be married, her dad telling her to be demure. 'You're not very demure,' says Alex. 'I grew up in the '50s and '60s,' says Lindy. 'Women were the losers in marriage back then.' They watch those scenes of the biker talking about feminism. Alex looks horrified, dismayed. But she listens to Lindy's responses and says, 'You got him, you got him there, because you're not fighting him, you're explaining to him.'

'You have to be sharp. You can't let them treat you badly,' says Lindy.

I fly home with my head full of her. Hours of conversation in which she has brought me up to date with her life now, with what really happened after the band broke up. She has told me what it has been like for her watching the band's memory being curated by others, watching the story of something she was part of for all those years harden into a different version, one from which she is partly excluded.

Being with her again for just a week has fired me up, and I arrive home even more determined to write her story. I can't bear the way she has become a minor character when she was one of the leads. When she walked into my life in 1983, she became my heroine. I saw her as a freedom fighter, forging a way ahead that others could follow.

And now I want to fight on her behalf.

Maybe, I think, it's a way I can pay her back.

PART FIVE

EX-WIVES

The reframing of The Go-Betweens as a duo, a partnership between Robert and Grant, begins very quickly
after the break-up. As early as 1991 Lindy and Amanda
write a letter to *Rolling Stone* objecting to a review of a
Go-Betweens compilation album which has largely overlooked their contributions. They don't mince their words.

'Of course, we knew The Go-Betweens was a two "man"
band,' they write.

> Our contributions (with a total of fourteen years) being
> the sexual partners to this team and providing them
> with subject matter for their songs. Naturally we were
> charmed to read ourselves described as 'an older woman'
> and 'naive young girl', not even worthy of being
> mentioned by name . . . History that has and continues
> to denigrate the great and ongoing contributions made
> by many women, once again, ensures that genuine talent
> is obscured . . .

The journalist who's written the review argues in his
defence that his piece had been brutally edited, removing

their names. He writes his own letter. He's a bit outraged. Of course he's not sexist. He refers to them sniggeringly as the 'wimmin'.

In 1997, at a music biz awards night, Lindy encounters the editor of a magazine who has just published an article saying that 'while some considered Morrison's drumming inspired, others suggested she was only there because she was the lover of Robert Forster'. Lindy, who describes herself as being 'out of my brains with anger', tells the editor he is stupid and doesn't understand art, then tips a glass of wine over him.

How can she not be bitter? When a collection of re-issues is released, a review describes them as 'this Antipodean duo, along with female drummer Lindy Morrison'. A trio, or even just a *band*, has become a duo with a drummer. She is peripheral, a hired hand.

And it's been so hard to leave it all behind. For years, she has dreams about the band, nightmares really, where they are on tour and can't find the stage, or they are lost and can't find the plane. In her sleep she is screaming at Robert and Grant, haunted by memories.

When Grant McLennan dies of a heart attack in 2006, aged forty-eight, it marks the complete end of The Go-Betweens, and Robert begins to idealise a friendship which was more intermittent, more complex, than he feels able to acknowledge. So that when, in 2016, he comes to write a book telling of the story of The Go-Betweens, he chooses to call it *Grant & I*, centring their friendship, and transforming the story of the band into the story of two friends.

The Go-Betweens are becoming mythologised – one of those 'best bands who never made it'. A review of a collection of reissues explicitly links them with the Velvet Underground and Big Star: 'each generation has their Go-Betweens, groups who encroach upon the fringes of popular taste without ever commanding the mass devotion their talents patently merit; groups for whom fame is a posthumous thing.'

It all makes Lindy laugh. She has no time for it. In certain moods, she can be utterly dismissive of the reverence for the band, and is at pains to point out that, however lauded they may have been, they sold barely any records. Sometimes she thinks it is only 'wanky journalists and some university students' who ever liked them.

This is bitterness talking as much as anything, words spoken while the wound is still raw. But the manner of the band's resurrection will only add to this bitterness. It makes her spiteful. She isn't always kind, or polite, when she encounters Robert, but what does he expect? That she'll just go quietly? Take all this on the chin? Let the band fly away to glory without her? Fuck that.

Time passes, and their star, their dead star, continues to rise. In their home town of Brisbane, a competition is held to rename the toll bridge over the river, and in September 2009 the winner is announced: the bridge will henceforth be known as the Go Between Bridge.

In 2018 a documentary film about the band is released. *Right Here* is directed by Kriv Stenders, an award-winning Australian film director with at least one box office smash hit, *Red Dog*, under his belt. Not every band gets a film made about them, and certainly not every band who never really made it. It's an achievement, an honour even, another marker that they have become one of those posthumously respected bands, more feted now than in their lifetime.

The posters and trailer for the film appear; the teasing tagline reads: 'Three Decades. Two Friends. One Band.'

Something has happened between the act and its recording – a band which was a trio has become the story of two friends. What happened to Two Wimps and a Witch? Who decided that the witch could be written out of the history, and who was at that meeting?

I go to see the film, anxious on Lindy's behalf, and from the very opening scenes it is clear that we are viewing events through Robert's eyes, through the lens of his memory. His is the first voice we hear, the first face we see, as he walks down a dusty road carrying a guitar case. He looks weathered but elegant, tall and troubled, and he stares into the middle distance and says, 'I don't have to use my imagination, I just have to remember.' We see whose film this is, whose memories these are.

It is not until seventeen minutes into the film, after Robert has talked about them wanting a female drummer – 'the perfect combination of three people,' he says, 'is two men and a woman, or two women and a man' – that Lindy makes her entrance. Three black-and-white pictures appear on screen. In the first she is sitting in a garden chair wearing a vintage '40s-style dress, a cup of tea balanced on her knee, her face in profile, short blonde hair curling into the nape of her neck. In the next she's standing, wearing the same dress, right hand on her hip, her elbow at a defiant angle, left arm raised and leaning against a shed door. And staring straight at the camera with a look on her face that can only be described as confrontational – chin slightly jutting, lips pouting, the eyes conveying a purely blunt 'Yeah? What YOU looking at?' In the final shot she's in a shirt and men's suit trousers.

Robert says, 'I'd seen Lindy, she was around, she was playing in a band called Zero – she was an actress too – social worker, drummer, actress, what a resumé! I was watching . . .' He mimes with his hand his eyes zooming in on her.

And as we watch the film our eyes do the same; they focus in on her, dragging her to the centre of the narrative – a narrative which attempts to treat her as a featured character, not a lead, but which finds that whenever she appears it is with a force that can't be repressed. She keeps breaking out of the box she's been put in. We see shots of the young band, and there is Lindy drumming, in full flight. Even in a still photograph she is in motion, bouncing on her drum stool, hair flying in her face – a source of energy, like their own personal generator at the back of the stage. She is the fuel, the battery pack. She is what turns them from *songwriters* into a *band*.

The Lindy of now appears on screen – short blonde bob, T-shirt and jeans, a smear of slightly smudged red lipstick – and she says of Robert, 'I've always loved intense nerdy men, they're my favourite sort of men – it wasn't difficult to fall in love with him,' and up flash two black-and-white photos of them, both naked, sitting in an old-fashioned free-standing bath tub full of bubbles.

Since she has appeared the film has come to life. Now two men will define her for us. The writer Gerard Lee is laughing as he says, 'Well, Lindy's larger than life – she's a bohemian goddess – you know, she works at the job of self-liberation,' and the camera zooms in on another bath shot, Robert and Lindy both looking straight to camera, a beautiful couple. The voice of journalist Clinton Walker on the soundtrack: 'Lindy is, as we know, this force of nature, and she's very attractive in that – and she can be a *fucking nightmare.*'

On the screen appears the video for 'Spring Rain', and Lindy is sitting in the rain, drumming in her dress, and on the soundtrack she says, with her trademark wide grin, 'It was wonderful – so I had to go and fuck it all up by breaking up with Robert. That's what I had to do, I had to mess it all up. Everything's going great, so why don't I break up with Robert?' She laughs. And the film cuts immediately to Clinton Walker who says, 'When Robert broke up with Lindy . . .'

Towards the end of the film there's an ominous sense of forces gathering, the climax approaching. A head full of steam is building up: heat, fury, disorder. An explosion seems to be the only thing that can bring the story to its end. The band are all exhausted and febrile. 'Tired and beat,' says Robert, and then, as if to dispel any sense that any of this was a big deal, he nonchalantly shrugs, says, 'That's the story,' and pops a grape in his mouth.

The dramatic break-up scene is coming, with Robert and Grant each summoning their female counterpart –

their mirror, their muse – in order to drop the bombshell. The Lindy of now and the Amanda of now sit together, looking at each other. Amanda speaks, confirming that she packed up and left as soon as Grant delivered the news, and Lindy, staring at her, says, 'Things were so broken, the trust was gone.' And Robert, in a separate room, looking back at that pivotal moment, that weird decision, delivers his self-exculpatory verdict: 'We were just bumbling boys.'

Those bumbling boys had, in fact, been men in their early thirties when they broke up the band. But, like children who can't be blamed for things they don't understand, men so often excuse their bad behaviour or have it excused for them. Robert and Grant are just boys who can't be expected to do any better. Male immaturity is an endless Get Out of Jail Free card.

As the film ends, with shots of Robert in front of a bonfire in the dark – the funeral pyre, the place where it all goes up in flames and ends in ashes – I think back to the moment in the film where Lindy, with controlled fury, distils her experience of being thrown out of the band. 'Both of us,' she says, 'refused to be defined as the girlfriends. And that's what they did when they dumped us – they treated us like ex-wives. And that was the greatest insult.'

When I see the film, it makes me angry, and then frustrated. How shortsighted, I think. Not to have recognised that Lindy was always one of their strongest assets. Which band would you rather go and see? Two Friends? Or Two Wimps and a Witch?

223

More than anything, I'm puzzled. Puzzled by the focus on the duo, which leaves out all the drama and tension in the tangle of the original trio, leaves out so much of what had been alluring. It's such a weakness, not to realise one of their great strengths.

The presence of Lindy had elevated them above the ranks of the stereotypical indie-boy-student band, connecting them with new currents in music which were overturning the gender imbalance. She provided a link with the late '70s feminist UK bands like the Au Pairs, Delta 5 and The Raincoats, a connection with the early '80s mixed-gender groups, and a look forward to the Riot Grrrl movement of the '90s.

Underplaying Lindy's contribution does not just do her a disservice: it is self-defeating. It makes them a less interesting band, saddling them with a dull identity when they had a bright and interesting one. It is their final act of self-sabotage. As Zadie Smith writes, in an essay on the artist Celia Paul, misogyny 'is a form of distortion, a way of not seeing'. Leaving a woman out of the story skews the perspective, gives you an alternate version – a more boring one.

Lindy had brought passion to the band, a tension between decorum and licence. Robert and Grant were cool, and she brought heat; they were calm and she brought energy; they were cerebral and she brought physicality. Without her, they were all decorum, all chasteness. She opened them up, picked them apart at the seams.

Even Robert, in his heart, knows the truth. In 2011 he publishes an essay collection entitled *The 10 Rules of Rock and Roll*, which includes a list of rules for bands to live by, all of them funny and all of them containing kernels of wisdom.

Rule number 10: 'The three-piece band is the purest form of rock and roll expression.'

But these are the ways in which the stories of women get told – in music, in art, in literature, in science. I think about the women who are silenced by encounters with disparaging, or predatory, men; the women who think they are working as equal partners only to find their names left off the credits; the women who work to their own rules and are then patronised for not knowing the real ones; and I remember how much sheer bloody determination it takes to keep forcing yourself back into the narrative, back to centre stage.

In his biography of the band, David Nichols writes that 'audience members at post-2000 Go-Betweens shows will still call out "Where's Lindy?"' I can only imagine how that must have stung the players left on the stage. And part of me is glad to hear about those audience members, and I'm grateful to them for not forgetting. It makes me feel that I'm not the only one who cares about this. That I'm not the only who missed her.

THE DRUMMER IS
THE BAND

'The Go-Betweens are my favourite band,' writes Jonathan Lethem, in an essay from 2001. It's just after they have reformed, without Lindy, to record a new album, *The Friends of Rachel Worth*. He has been asked to review it for *Rolling Stone*, but doesn't want to. In fact, he has strong feelings about not wanting to write or even think about the reunion, or have anything to do with the new album. Instead, he writes about his resistance to The Go-Betweens in their new incarnation. His resistance is all to do with the absence of Lindy.

This is where imagination kicks in, as it always does when we think about artists we love and wonder about their lives from the few details and clues we have. Lethem imagines that the friendship between Robert, Grant and Lindy is 'beautiful and complicated', and that it takes the form of a kind of love triangle.

I've always imagined that Robert Forster and Grant McLennan were each Lindy's boyfriend in turn, and that the difficulties and ambiguities of this long arrangement and disarrangement are the impenetrable knot at the core of the music, the mystery that keeps me coming back.

It's funny, because he's right that there was a love triangle, but while he imagines the two boys as rivals for Lindy's affection, the truth is that it was Grant and Lindy who never resolved their competition for Robert's esteem and attention. If Robert and Grant (in their dreams) were Lennon and McCartney, then Lindy was Yoko – the woman in between the two men, creative in her own right, disrupting their friendship.

The centrepiece of Lethem's essay is a description of a Go-Betweens gig in Berkeley, California, in the late '80s. The crowd at the local rock venue consists of about 'twenty-five or thirty people, a loosely packed herd of worshippers, but our worship couldn't console The Go-Betweens, not this night'.

The gig sounds like it comes towards the end of a disastrous tour, at the point when the band were disintegrating. Tension on stage, a palpable sense that anger and resentment have replaced shared ambition and camaraderie, 'and Lindy, the drummer, the original Go-Between, had been drinking. Really drinking, so she was lurching and obvious and couldn't keep time.'

In her flat, in 2019, I sit and read the piece to her. I want her reaction. I want to know if any of it is true.

'Oh yeah, it's definitely true. I know what happened that day. I had been drinking gin martinis with my brother's American family, from when he'd been an exchange student. I had no idea how strong they were and I got so smashed I didn't know what I was doing. I remember being in the van driving there, and I was just incoherent – it must have been obvious to everyone that I wasn't gonna be able to play. I must've been playing so badly.'

Here she pauses, and then shrieks with laughter.

'Everyone was really furious with me before we even started, 'cause I'd turned up so smashed.'

It's obvious to Lethem that the other band members are furious with her. The whole band look miserable.

They made it through a song, argued again, and then Lindy stormed off, between the two singers, toward the bar. She weaved. At the bar she got something – another drink? Water? Carrying it she lurched back to the stage, and as she moved through the crowd she brushed me, a butt-against-lap swipe, the kind which happens late at night at crazy parties, when intentions are blurry. I know this seems ridiculous, but it happened. She was taunting one or both of the men onstage by making physical contact with men in the audience, and in the small, loosely populated room it was apparent that it was having an effect, though what sort I wouldn't presume to say. The horrible intimacy, the unexpected access to the band's unhappiness, was wrenching. It was also terribly sexy – I learned something that night about how vivid a smashed woman can be.

'Is that really what happened?' I ask her.

'I don't remember the swaying my hips into him, or whatever . . . but it's probably true.' She laughs again.

'I probably was taunting them. Things were already so tense between us by then – and you know, I'd got drunk, and I'd put up with all their shenanigans over the years – and I guess I thought it was my turn to play up, and I was just gonna play it up to the hilt. I was so drunk I didn't care. I would've been flirtatious with the men in the audience, yeah, it would've been so much fun, I would've thought it was hilarious – I was having the time of my life!'

Lethem breaks his promise not to buy the record by the newly reformed Go-Betweens. He can't help himself, can't resist. So he buys it, and puts it on in the car, and starts crying. He can't bear it; everything about it reminds him of her loss.

And here's the crux of his piece: it isn't about love triangles, it's about drummers.

> There's something I've always liked about Led Zeppelin's refusal to exist for even one minute after John Bonham's death. And I'd always felt the opposite about The Who – that they betrayed their audience by carrying on after Keith Moon . . . I mean, songwriters come and go, but the drummer is the band.

The drummer is the band.

Like a heartbeat, a pulse, if the drummer stops, everything stops. The band flatlines.

That night, when Lethem saw them, Lindy's energy was out of control. The currents flowing between the members of the band were disrupted, or blocked. Signals weren't getting through. The connections weren't being made. The centre couldn't hold.

She was like a heart that had gone into atrial fibrillation, her electricity all wrong.

Lethem concludes by saying that, yes, he will play this new record, and might end up liking it, but he won't write about it because: 'I'm carrying a torch for Lindy. Her name isn't even in the thank-yous. There's a story there, I know there is . . .'

'I mean the whole story is appalling, if you're talking about being a professional performer, but as an anecdote in relation to rock 'n ' roll, it is what it is – I'm smashed on stage. The fact that I get to leave and go to the bar is incredible.

'I was probably playing out of time – and they would've been so angry – and I'm sure I just thought it was so unfair. Over the years Robert had been out of it on pain-killers and alcohol, Grant had had his nights on drugs – everyone had had a turn at playing up. One night in Holland, we couldn't find Robert to go on stage, and he was found in a toilet, huddled and paranoid from smoking pot.

'So I don't know why I got into so much trouble, but I did, I got into real trouble with them.

'And then I fell off the stage and sprained my ankle.

'At the end of the night I was sitting with my foot in an ice bucket, sobbing.

'Everything about that night was terrible.'

'The thing is,' I say, 'what comes out of this piece is that he is on your side, he carries a torch for you.'

I read again the bit about him not wanting to listen to the band without Lindy. 'Listen to what he says: "the drummer is the band". It's amazing!'

She laughs at that – and her tone is gentle now – a mixture of regret and gratitude. 'Ah, that's great. My behaviour was abominable, but it's such a great rock 'n' roll story. The thing is, I NEVER did that, never got smashed and acted like that on stage. And the one night it happens there's a writer in the audience!!

'CAN YOU BELIEVE IT?'

MINOR CHARACTERS

In 1988 I write a letter to Lindy about a new song I have written, knowing she'll understand.

> I have a new song called 'Me and Bobby D', a critique of male heroes a la Bob Dylan and Kerouac. R Forster will hate it. Or maybe he won't, but G McLennan surely will. I remember that argument one night at our old flat, with you versus the boys on the subject of good ol' Bobby D.

I've been inspired by Joyce Johnson's book *Minor Characters*, which she published in 1983. It's a memoir of her time spent with the heroes of the Beat generation – Jack Kerouac, Allen Ginsberg and so on – and how the women involved in that scene, drawn to the same unconventional freedoms as those rebellious men, ended up relegated to the roles of muse and helpmeet, and thus were cast as minor characters in the story of their own lives.

The song I write expresses my feelings about revered male artists and the women who fall into their shadow. I had loved *On the Road* as a teen, and I can still remember how deeply I was drawn to its portrayal of freedom, its dreams of transcendence. As Johnson writes: 'Naturally, we fell in love with men who were rebels. We fell very quickly, believing they would take us along on their journeys and adventures.'

Johnson is already a writer herself when she becomes Kerouac's lover at the moment when his career takes flight. She has women friends who write their own poetry, make their own sculptures, but one of them declines to read her poetry out loud, telling herself that, unlike her man's, it isn't good enough. 'Some of it *was* good enough, she'll admit fiercely, years later.' The woman who sculpts is the wife of a photographer, and in the evenings puts away her work to tend to the children and 'slice the vegetables' often seeming 'distracted, almost sullen'. Who can blame her?

Johnson herself gets a deal from Random House to publish her first novel, but just then, *On the Road* takes the world by storm. Kerouac's editor brings champagne on the morning of his life-changing review from the *New York Times*, and when Kerouac drinks the lot, the editor takes Johnson aside as he leaves the apartment and says to her urgently, 'Take care of this man.'

She keeps working as a secretary while she finishes her novel, which reminds me of Lindy working as a cleaner. Johnson writes: 'It was all right for women to go out and earn wages, since they had no important creative endeavours to be distracted from. The women didn't mind, or, if they did, they never said – not until years later.'

By the time I write 'Me and Bobby D', I've become embittered by the notion that we should hang on the coattails of these Great Male Artists, embarrassed perhaps by how much I had fallen into that trap when younger. It's a tart and sour little song that I write, and what it really expresses is jealousy.

And what I don't know at the time, when I write to tell Lindy about my song, is that she herself will be turned into a minor character in her own story; that this same erasure will happen to her. That it will also, from time to time, happen to me, for instance in an album review headline describing me as a '55-year-old wife and mother', rather than a '55-year-old writer and singer'. My creative identity vanishes and is replaced by a description of my domestic status. My previous work disappears, and the reviewer allows himself to be pleasantly surprised by my charming achievements.

This is the way we are patronised. This is the way we vanish.

Johnson concludes her book by recalling how thrilled she had been to be part of the Beat scene, how exciting it had been to have a 'seat at the table in the exact centre of the universe, that midnight place where so much is converging, the only place in America that's alive . . .' And yet she knows now that

> as a female, she's not quite part of this convergence. A fact she ignores, sitting by in her excitement as the voices of the men, always the men, passionately rise and fall . . . Merely being here, she tells herself, is enough.

In writing the book, she says: 'what I refuse to relinquish is her expectancy. It's only her silence that I wish finally to give up.' Her book undoes that silence and reveals what a talented author she is in her own right. As Angela Carter says: 'This is the muse's side of the story. It turns out the muse could write as well as anybody.'

I find myself wondering about Lindy and all that time she spent hanging around two songwriters without writing songs herself. I imagine the kind of songs she might have written, I think of things she has said and picture them as lyrics, sung in the kind of no-fucks-given voice that we love from women songwriters these days.

There are lines you could sing.

Like: *We'd meet on the stairs for a glamorous fuck.*

Or: *The days are endless, it's so bright / until 9 p.m. and for a while / I simply sat in bars until 6 a.m. / because it felt like it was only midnight.*

Or: *Every time you mention (him) my heart lets me know again: There's no one like him here, for sure.*

Or even, yelled at full volume, in a feminist punk band: *I was sitting on his cock / working out our lives together.*

I know, I know; she's never wanted to write songs, and she should be given her full due in the story anyway, for being the drummer she has always been. But I can't help thinking of the voices we miss, the art that doesn't happen, the work that women don't make because they underestimate themselves.

In an essay entitled 'Grandmother Spider', Rebecca Solnit writes about 'obliteration', about the different ways in which women disappear. She describes how they vanish from family trees as the lineage passes from father to son, and then looks at how the same thing has happened in art history 'when we were told that Picasso begat Pollock and Pollock begat Warhol and so it went, as though artists were influenced only by other artists'.

Other forms of 'female nonexistence', she says, include women being told to stay home to avoid rape, disappearing off the streets, or taking their husband's name and passing it on to their child, their own name being lost. And she connects all these ideas through an artwork called *Spiderweb* by Ana Teresa Fernández, summoning up images of grandmother spiders spinning narratives and artworks, telling their stories while also being caught in the web.

And I have carried with me all the way through the writing of this book this particular line from Solnit's essay as a template for what I've tried to do, the way in which I want to reclaim Lindy's story, to save it before it's too late and to add it to all the other lost stories.

To spin the web and not be caught in it, to create the world, to create your own life, to rule your own fate, to name the grandmothers as well as the fathers, to draw nets and not just straight lines, to be a maker as well as a cleaner, to be able to sing and not be silenced, to take down the veil and appear: all these are the banners on the laundry line I hang out.

Why does it matter that Lindy has been partly written out of the story of the band? Because it happens all the time. Every time I see a music documentary where only men speak, even though the band's fans were teenage girls; every time I see a festival bill with no women on the stages; every time I read an account from which half the names seem to be missing – something in me rises up, tense and snarling, and it looks very like fury.

The Go-Betweens weren't the biggest band in the world. You might never have heard of them. But they had their moment in the limelight, their hour upon the stage. They were reviewed and interviewed, recorded and filmed. Their work is now collected in lush box sets, a movie tells their history, a bridge bears their name. It's not nothing, by any means.

And perhaps Lindy's part in that is a tiny story. Taken individually, each of our stories is tiny. But taken together, they form an epic. One that repeats, over and over again. We were there, we existed, we played our part. And every retelling is a small step towards redressing the balance.

I WANT EVERYTHING

So here we are.

Lindy and I, we've lived different lives, but with moments of intense connection and times when our similarities have outweighed anything else. Both of us have wrestled with the idea of how to stay independent and have come to different conclusions. Back when I was twenty-six, and already in a committed relationship, I wrote down in my notebook that quote from de Beauvoir about living both with and apart from a lover. And Deborah Levy, in *The Cost of Living*, quotes de Beauvoir, in a letter to Nelson Algren: 'I want everything from life, I want to be a woman and to be a man, to have many friends and have loneliness, to work much and write good books and to travel and enjoy myself . . .'

Amen to that. The competing demands of independence and love, how do we resolve them? Each in our own way. Lindy and I, we've done our best; we've done OK.

I read Suzanne Moore's tribute to Deborah Orr after her death in October 2019, and it reads like something I might have written about Lindy. 'Men were scared of her but also absolutely compelled by her . . . God was she difficult, though, and I won't pretend otherwise. She would turn up at dinner parties with a bottle of whisky, drink it and berate the host . . . In all her complicated glory she was wild. Untamed. Never not true to herself. "Who among us can say that?"'

Lindy can, I think. The end of The Go-Betweens, she said, 'was pivotal in me going out and establishing myself as Lindy Morrison, and I will not be anyone but Lindy Morrison, and nothing will change that'.

So this is what I offer. A version of her life. My outsider/insider view of her, and of us. This is how it seemed to me.

I look at their album covers, and so often she is the one making eye contact with the viewer. On the first album, *Send Me a Lullaby*, paintings of the three of them show Grant looking down and Robert looking towards Lindy, while she is staring challengingly outwards, not directly at us, but at someone or something just over our shoulder. Defiant, full of confidence, as usual.

I find some footage on YouTube of the band playing a song called 'Your Turn, My Turn' in Bradford in 1983. The camera is close in on Lindy for the intro, and she is sultry, with huge dark eyes, then suddenly a drumstick flies out of her hand. She grimaces, grins, grabs another one and carries on. Unstoppable.

I leaf through a folder full of photos, and from thirty-five years ago she looks out at me, smiling and relaxed with short auburn-tinged hair. How very beautiful she is. In a sheet of contact prints she is crop-haired and wearing a boy's V-neck jumper and jeans, gripping a standard lamp topped with a bare lightbulb as if it were a microphone stand. She's laughing in every picture, enjoying the antic nonsense of it all. Another set of photos and she is on her own, holding drumsticks and leaning against a bass drum case. In another picture, the whole band – the boys in suit jackets, Lindy in a tight T-shirt and jeans, languidly smoking. In another, she's playing the drums, mid-action, a look of intense concentration on her face, hair in her eyes, drumsticks a blur.

In every picture she leaps out, somehow both vulnerable and true. The bare bulbs around the mirror throw her eyes into shade, light up her golden hair. I want to know more. I wonder what she's thinking. I wonder whether she'll like me back.

I wonder what perfume she's wearing. What lipstick.

NO FILTER

January 2019

I've been so remiss. We haven't spoken in years. God, how many years, I ask myself. Could it be twenty? Could it really be that long? I open Skype and hit the connection and it makes those alien bleeping noises that sound like you're calling outer space, although it's true that I am dialling up the other side of the world and a whole other period of my life, one I'd thought long dead.

You answer, grinning as always, and you look just as I knew you would. I'm in a hotel room and you're in your office at home, shelves of books on the wall behind you, and a Go-Betweens poster, an old one, from the days when you were a four-piece. You are peering at the screen, the way you always do. I'm never sure whether it's still a left-over from the short-sightedness, or just the Australian squint that comes as a result of growing up under that dazzling sun, that diamond brightness.

Within minutes you are talking both to me and at me, in that stream-of-consciousness style you've always had, which you describe as 'having no filter', and which soothing and overwhelming, but always fascinating, always engaging. You start, entirely in character, talking about

241

your appearance, but over the course of an hour give me a crash course in the current state of your life.

You point to your hair, a neat blonde bob. 'I'm doing Byron Bay surfer girl!' you begin. 'A while ago, I was spending time on stage with twenty-five- and thirty-year-olds so I thought I had to update my image. But now I think I can go back to being appropriate to my dotage . . . I'll never have long hair again. It's totally inappropriate in a woman past her fifties . . . the new feminism, which I describe as the new puritanism . . . I told you about the letters I wrote to myself when I was thirteen or fourteen? I know I have them somewhere. There's a red box. I can't remember seeing it for a few years. I'll have a look for it at the weekend . . . I had a really passionate affair with Denis Walker from the Black Panther movement, and the effects of that . . . truly catastrophic . . . the book has to appeal to more than just the three German student fans The Go-Betweens have . . . the reader likes to hear about relationships, and more and more women are interested in hearing about relationships between women . . . I always had faith, Tracey, in my work, particularly my early work, which was so interesting . . . Don't you think you get very cautious as you get older? I'm not wild like I used to be, in any way . . . No, really I'm not. I can't be . . .'

I'm laughing by now, and 'Oh well, we'll see,' I think. And in the next sentence you tell me three more things:

1. You are pissed off at a friend for measuring out your gin;

242

2. You have been spending your days at a nudist beach;

3. It is your current party piece to tell the story of being wronged by a film director.

As you're talking, the years vanish, slinking out of the room unnoticed. It was yesterday that we last chatted like this, and I cooked you dinner, and then we went to the cinema, and talked about men and books and sex, and you were outrageous, and I loved it. And I think to myself, 'It *is* a shame, yeah, that you're not wild any more. How straight you've become. How boring.' And I laugh and shake my head.

We talk about this idea I have for a book, and you're intrigued, but also concerned about how I'm going to make sense of any of it. How much I want to know. What you should tell me.

Through a laptop screen, we look at each other from opposite sides of the world. You are a long way away, untouchable but still recognisable. Your face, my face. Reflections in a mirror. Opposites, the same. I tell you that making sense of the story is my problem. You needn't worry about that. Your role is simple.

'Just tell me EVERYTHING,' I say. 'Be indiscreet. I can be discreet later.'

And so we begin.

POSTSCRIPT

An email, 6 September 2019, the day I leave Sydney:

It's been great fun having you here.
What a bloody adventure. Like a lifetime.
Lindy

BIBLIOGRAPHY

David Nichols – *The Go-Betweens*. Verse Chorus Press, 2003.

Andrew Stafford – *Pig City: From the Saints to Savage Garden*. University of Queensland Press, 2014.

Donald Horne – *The Lucky Country*. Penguin Group (Australia), 2008.

Gerard Lee – *True Love and How to Get It*. University of Queensland Press, 1986.

John Pilger – *A Secret Country*. Vintage, 1992.

Robert Forster – *Grant & I: Inside and Outside the Go-Betweens*. Omnibus Press, 2018.

Layne Redmond – *When the Drummers Were Women: A Spiritual History of Rhythm*. Echo Point Books & Media, 2018.

Rebecca Solnit – 'Grandmother Spider' in *Men Explain Things to Me*. Granta, 2014.

Jonathan Lethem – 'Open Letter to Stacy (The Go-Betweens)' in *The Ecstasy of Influence: Nonfictions, etc.* Vintage, 2013.

Sam Watson – 'Equal and Opposite Forces' in Edwina Shaw (editor), *Bjelke Blues: Stories of Repression and Resistance in Joh Bjelke-Petersen's Queensland 1968–1987*. AndAlso Books, 2019.

Joyce Johnson – *Minor Characters: A Beat Memoir*. Penguin Books, 1999.

Deborah Levy – *The Cost of Living*. Penguin Books, 2019.

Kim Addonizio – *Wild Nights: New & Selected Poems*. Bloodaxe Books, 2015.

'To a photograph of the field officer' essay by Lindy in Marieke Hardy and Michaela McGuire (curators), *Women of Letters*. Viking, 2011.

'Stranded' essay by Lindy in Sybil Nolan (editor), *The Dismissal: Where were you on November 11, 1975?* Melbourne University Press, 2015.

'Brisbane in the late 70s was fast and furious' article by Lindy in *Guardian*, 8 September 2018.

ACKNOWLEDGEMENTS

Thanks above all to Lindy Morrison.

And also to Peter Walsh, Kate Wilson, Diana Priest, Trevor Stuart, Amanda Brown, Sam Watson, Matthew Cooper, Jonathan Turner, Bob Johnson, Pete Paphides, Geoffrey Titley, Ben Watt, Kirsty McLachlan, Francis Bickmore, Vicki Rutherford, Leila Cruickshank, Alison Rae, Jess Neale, Jenny Fry, Vicki Watson, Katie Huckstep, Megan Reid.

PERMISSION CREDITS